DATING,
MATING,
AND
RELATING

Albert Ellis has authored or edited 70 books. Some of his most important books for the public and the psychology professional include:

How to Live With a Neurotic
Sex Without Guilt
The Art and Science of Love
A Guide to Rational Living (with Robert A. Harper)
The Encyclopedia of Sexual Behavior
Reason and Emotion in Psychotherapy
Executive Leadership
How to Master Your Fear of Flying
Humanistic Psychotherapy: The Rational—Emotive Approach
A Guide to Personal Happiness (with Irving Becker)
Clinical Applications of Rational–Emotive Approach (with Michael
    Bernard)
Overcoming Resistance
*How to Stubbornly Refuse to Make Yourself Miserable About
    Anything—Yes, Anything!*
Rational–Emotive Couples Therapy (with Joyce Sichel, Raymond
    Yeager, Dominic Di Mattia, and Raymond Di Giuseppe)
How to Keep People From Pushing Your Buttons (with Arthur Lange)
What to Do When AA Doesn't Work (with Emmett Velten)
Better, Deeper, and More Enduring Brief Therapy
Stress Counseling: A Rational Emotive Behavior Approach (with Jack
    Gordon, Michael Neenan, and Stephen Palmer
How to Control Your Anger Before It Controls You
    (with R.C. Tafrate)
Optimal Aging (with Emmett Veltan)
The Albert Ellis Reader (with Shawn Blau)
How to Make Yourself Happy and Remarkably Less Disturbable
The Secret of Overcoming Verbal Abuse (with Grad Powers)
Feeling Better, Getting Better, and Staying Better
Overcoming Destructive Beliefs, Feeling, and Behaviors
Counseling and Psychotherapy With Religious Persons (with Stevan L.
    Nielson and W. Brad Johnson)

Robert A. Harper is the author of several books, including:

Marriage
Problems of American Society (with John F. Cuber and William F.
    Kenkel)
Psychoanalysis and Psychotherapy

DATING, MATING, AND RELATING

How to Build a Healthy Relationship

Albert Ellis, Ph.D.
and
Robert A. Harper, Ph.D.

CITADEL PRESS
Kensington Publishing Corp.
www.kensingtonbooks.com

CITADEL PRESS BOOKS are published by

Kensington Publishing Corp.
850 Third Avenue
New York, NY 10022

Previously published as *How to Stop Destroying Your Relationships*

All Kensington titles, imprints, and distributed lines are available at special quantity discounts for bulk purchases for sales promotions, premiums, fund-raising, educational, or institutional use. Special book excerpts or customized printings can also be created to fit specific needs. For details, write or phone the office of the Kensington special sales manager: Kensington Publishing Corp., 850 Third Avenue, New York, NY 10022, attn: Special Sales Department, phone 1-800-221-2647.

CITADEL PRESS and the Citadel logo are Reg. U.S. Pat. & TM Off.

First printing: January 2003

10 9 8 7 6 5 4 3 2 1

Printed in the United States of America

Library of Congress Control Number: 2002113381

ISBN 0-8065-2454-5

To Janet L. Wolfe and Mimi Harper,
who have rationally tolerated us as their mates for lo,
these many years.
Affectionately and lovingly,

A.E.
R.A.H.

Contents

Preface

Do we have the right to pen a *new* book on dating, mating, and relating? Well, yes—in fact, we do. Both of us have worked for decades in the sex/marriage/family (SMF) field—teaching, counseling, writing, and speaking. Both of us are pioneers in liberal and democratic approaches to SMF problems, sometimes to our detriment. Largely because of our full-time business as psychologists we have never undertaken a revision of our 1961 book, *A Guide to Successful Marriage*. For all its usefulness and continued popularity, changes in the four decades since the book appeared have made a revision seem inadequate. Instead, we decided to produce a new and different book on how two people can intimately relate, mainly—though it may sound odd—for their own sheer enjoyment.

In this book, we use the word "intimate" to refer simply to a "close personal relationship," not to indicate a sexual relationship. You and your partner may have a close relationship though nothing erotic has ever occurred between you, while another couple, even if they copulate extensively, may never develop real intimacy. We will focus on your achieving and maintaining intimacy in a close relationship, whether you are married or single, having sex or not, heterosexual or homosexual. The close relationships we will look at are those in which people are married or living together in an intimate, and not merely sexual, relationship. We will show you how when a close personal relationship of yours falters or fails, the relationship itself is rarely entirely to blame. We shall explore not only the nature of your problems, but ways of alleviating them.

As we try to be in our relationship therapy, so in this book we will strive to be even-handed and nonjudgmental in our approach. We will look at several types of couples: young and older, gay and straight; and show how overcoming difficulties in close personal relationships is similar to handling individual problems. So try to learn from the variety of couples presented. Don't pass over those that seem foreign to you, as the relationship and its problems might be closer to your own than you expect.

What we emphasize first and foremost is choice. Our mission is to help two (or more) people to relate more interestingly and enjoyably to one another—but only *if they so choose.* You are free to decide to relate to other people or not at all. No one *must* learn to function well in couplehood, but we have found that an overwhelming majority of people do want to learn how to do so.

While couples and families normally live with other people, couples are the main focus of this book. However, in many instances, close personal relationships include more than two people, so we have included chapters on getting along together and with others, including friends, in-laws, and children. We look closely at couples, remembering that we are not dealing with a mystical "relationship" but with two interacting *individuals.* The individual is key to the relationship, because only by working on him or herself does each individual improve his or her interaction.

Fun is a great ingredient in a close relationship, so we even try, while endorsing this concept, to have some fun ourselves. In our rational emotive behavior therapy (REBT) philosophy, long-term enjoyment of life is what makes sense. We hope you find such long-term satisfaction and your own sparkling happy couple in the process.

Cheers,

Albert Ellis, Ph.D.
Albert Ellis Institute
New York City

Robert A. Harper, Ph.D.
Washington, D.C.

DATING,
MATING,
AND
RELATING

1

Getting Relationships Together by Getting Yourself Together

Newborn infants often panic when a newspaper or a paper bag is rustled near their ears. To them, with their near-zero experience with the non-uterine world, any sudden change in the messages impinging on their senses may represent a great threat. As experiences increase, so may real or imagined dangers. Some dangers lessen or disappear, but others increase. As the eight-year-old shows when he or she hides in the closet at a thunderclap, experience does not necessarily teach one how to deal with fear.

How can you learn to live a relatively unpanicked life? How can you tolerate the frustrations of coupling? Not easily! Most of us learn to face crackling paper and even thunder without fear, but we tend to pick up other disturbances that interrupt our individual happiness and render us undelightful to another person who wants to keep closely relating.

Before you contemplate and get involved in couplehood, you had better keep two things in the back of your mind. First, you must make substantial headway in accepting and coping with your own life. Second, be sure to look for long-term satisfactions—not just immediate gratifications.

We emphasize coupling when we deal with happiness-seeking

not because we believe that true and lasting enjoyment cannot be achieved by solitary individuals—both history and current observation prove that it can be—but because humans try, and often try repeatedly, to be in happily intimate relationships. Also, our long experience as scientists, educators, and clinicians indicates that most of us can use all the help we can get in learning how to couple happily.

We developed the Rational Emotive Behavior Therapy (REBT) theory of human behavior in the mid-1950s. This theory holds that people are born with strong tendencies to act both well (self-helpfully) and badly (self-defeatingly), but that they have considerable choice in the way they react. You, as a human, are born with two conflicting tendencies: a tendency to needlessly (and, hence, neurotically) disturb yourself, and a tendency to seek enjoyable, non-disturbed thoughts, feelings, and behaviors. REBT tries to help you to enhance the positive second tendency and to reduce the strength and persistence of the first, which is often reinforced by yourself and by others.

Before we get to the major principles of REBT and how to apply them to your life, let us present some basic facts about humans and human behavior.

First off, all human behavior (thinking, perceiving, feeling, and acting) derives from individuals. No proof has ever been uncovered of a collective unconscious, let alone a collective conscious. Also, there is no such thing as a mystical couple merged into one being. Therefore, you have to make efforts at changing a relationship first within yourself. Then you have to *agree* with your partner that you will do or not do certain things to improve your relationship, and vice versa. But whatever middle ground you come to as a couple, your actions or inactions (and the attitudes behind them) still belong to you (Individual A) and to your partner (Individual B) separately.

Keeping that in mind, know that you can only directly change yourself. Even if you are a therapist, all you can do is try to make change seem attractive and interesting and possible for someone else—it's up to the individual whether or not s/he makes the change.

If you think you can change Individual B or that s/he automatically *should* change (because, after all, look how wonderfully changed *you* are), trouble will likely ensue!

Individuals function more effectively and enjoyably when they learn to reduce their tendency—either instilled early on or possibly innate—to rate themselves. Contrary to many other psychotherapists and educators, we have long contended that self-esteem is something to shun rather than to embrace and enhance. By all means take satisfaction in your behavior—your thoughts, feelings, perceptions, and actions—and rate or have your behavior rated by others as "good" or "bad." But rating your personhood, your totality, your self is bound to be incomplete and inaccurate. Is a "good person" always "good" and therefore a "good" hockey player, orator, or electronic troubleshooter all at once? *Self*-ratings can have distracting and disturbing effects. If you are focused on "How am I as a person?" or *"Am* I what others rate me to be?" you are probably reducing the effectiveness of what you are *doing* to that degree. Self-rating leads to self-cremating.

The next principle is a tough one to understand and difficult to act on in your daily life, as most of us have been immersed in the process of rating the total person (ourselves and others) since infancy. "She's a good baby." "I'm a bad person." Many of the efforts of REBT are directed toward helping people overcome their tendencies to rate themselves and others as persons, and instead only to evaluate actions. By rating people's actions, separate from their personhood, we can learn to live more happily.

Let's step back for a moment to examine the ABCs of REBT. *A* stands for the activating events or adversities in your life—the phone is ringing, your jury duty notice has arrived, or your life raft has developed a leak. *B* is your beliefs or belief system, or how you filter the *A*'s. *C* is for consequences (usually emotional) and is a result of how you used *B* to deal with *A*. Like most people, you probably thought that A (adversities) produces C (consequences) directly and naturally. But that isn't necessarily the case. REBT teaches you to understand that your Bs largely effect your Cs. Let us illustrate.

Charlene, an intelligent and energetic fifteen-year-old, sought therapy because, in her words: "I have just squarely faced the fact that I am a lesbian, and naturally it blows my mind. What a shit I am for letting myself be attracted to *women*. I've known about my lesbianism for a long time, but I kept telling myself that it would blow over—it was a phase I was going through. Now I'm looking at it—I'm a total goddamned dyke. And it's terrible, and I hate it! I am miserable. I don't want to live, but my mother, who doesn't know what's eating me but knows something is, made me come to see you. I know it won't do a damned bit of good. I want to fucking well die." Dr. Harper had several REBT sessions with Charlene. Here is an excerpt from one of their sessions.

R.A.H.: Charlene, of course, you have the right to die, but dying is an irrevocable decision. Since you have gone to the trouble of coming here, let's look at some of the assumptions you are making. While it's possible that you may not be lesbian, let's assume for the time being that you are. Why do you think being a lesbian makes you a shit?

Charlene: Well, doesn't it? Anybody who wants to be normal and get married and have kids and be respected in the community and ends up a dyke ends up a shit. Ask anybody—except maybe another dyke.

R.A.H.: Your exception tells me that you don't necessarily believe that a lesbian *must* be and *must* feel herself to be a shit. So you grant the possibility that a lesbian does not *have* to rate herself negatively and go around feeling miserable.

Charlene: Yeah, but this is all theoretical crud. The *fact* is that I'm a dyke and I don't want to be and I think I'm a shit and I'd rather die than go on this way.

R.A.H.: Please understand that I fully accept you as a person who has an undeniable right to feel however you choose to feel. That's the concept: *choice*. And by this I mean a *practical* choice, not just some way-out theoretical choice.

Charlene: You mean I can choose whether to be a lesbian or not?

R.A.H.: Possibly that, too. But we are right now accepting the assumption that you are a lesbian, and we are challenging your assumption that this makes you a shit. Because you understandably want results and not a philosophical discussion at this point, close your eyes, please. Now think, "I am a lesbian," and tell me what you are feeling.

Charlene: What I've already told you: shitty, terrible, miserable, like dying.

R.A.H.: Okay. Keeping your eyes closed, think, "I am a lesbian," but see if you can *feel* any differently about it.

Charlene: Oh, come on. You're treating me like a stupid child.

R.A.H.: It probably seems that way to you, but *I* think I am accepting you as a full person who has developed some heavy self-downing ways and could use a little help in easing up on it. So what have you got to lose? Please close your eyes again and think, "I am a lesbian." Now see if you can feel less miserable about it.

Charlene (after several silent minutes and with eyes still closed): Well, maybe now I feel like yeah, I'm a lesbian, but maybe it's not the end of the world. I suppose I don't have to die, but I still see a pretty shitty life for myself compared with what I'd thought I would be: a beautiful and brilliant young physician who is also a perfect wife and mother to a perfect husband and three perfect children. To say the least, I feel disappointed. *(She opens her eyes and gives a rather sickly smile.)*

R.A.H.: Splendid! You have quickly moved from *despair* to feeling *disappointment*. There is a world of difference: In despair, as you know, all hope is gone; in disappointment, no matter how crushed and discouraged you feel, hope creeps back in. Tell me, how did you change your feelings?

Charlene: I'm not sure, but I think the way you reacted to me showed me that it was at least worth *trying* to feel differently about being a lesbian. As I tried I thought about how *you* weren't treating me like a shit—so maybe I wasn't entirely a shit. But I also thought about a number of people who are lesbians and who don't despair about it. They're not blowing their brains out or jumping in front of a train.

R.A.H.: Very good again! You realize that your self-acceptance was encouraged by my unconditional acceptance of you as a person, but that was not the whole reason your self-feelings started to change. You began to think of some other people and their behavior, which cast some doubt on your earlier conviction that lesbianism and shithood are synonymous. Are you also starting to see how what you think and what you *feel* are so mixed up in each other that it becomes hard to distinguish one from the other?

Charlene: Yeah, I suppose if I *think* I'm a shit for being a dyke, I'm going to *feel* like a shit. Which, by the way, I still do. I just don't feel all's necessarily lost.

R.A.H.: That is progress. None of us completely transforms his/her behavior in one easy lesson. To change even the simplest thoughts, feelings, and actions often takes long, hard, and persistent work. But that's life—and it's not awful.

Through her comments about thinking and feeling, Charlene indicated she was already beginning to understand the fundamentals of the ABCs of REBT: namely, that her beliefs about lesbianism and not the activating event of her "discovery" of her sexual disposition led to her feelings (consequences). Dr. Harper indicated to her, however, this fine beginning did not mean that Charlene would not have a long and difficult learning process ahead. While she saw this, she also saw that it might work, so we continued working on the ABCs of her feelings and on her understanding and challenging her self-rating process.

By gradually learning to make better judgments about her thoughts, feelings, actions, and perceptions—her behavior—*instead* of making judgments about her total self or personhood, Charlene chose this solution to the problem of self-downing. No person can be shown to be, as a person, good or bad. Either way is an unprovable assumption. However, you will feel miserable if you assume that you *are* bad (at the core no damned good), and you'll feel much better if you assume that you're okay—that is, a satisfactory human being. Why not make the assumption that makes you feel better?

"*But,*" Charlene said at first (like many of our clients do), "it is no assumption that I am a shitty person. I really am." Over and over again we had to help her see that she was accepting an arbitrary and unprovable judgment as indisputable and unchangeable, and that was a *choice* she was making. She could, as I kept pointing out, learn to dispute such a nonsensical and destructive judgment of herself and gradually (with diligent persistence) substitute a more positive self-rating.

As REBT therapists we are never wholly satisfied with what we call the inelegant, but workable, solution chosen by Charlene. Why? Because we are quite aware that positive self-evaluations are readily reversible. If you become convinced you are a good person for any reason except "because I exist," that reason can be snatched away, and you can be left again with the old conviction that you are somehow inadequate, unacceptable, undesirable, inferior, or "bad" because you were not able to achieve whatever you had decided you *had* to achieve to be "good."

We believe, however, that if you work hard at challenging your self-downing judgments, substituting positive judgments, and deciding, "I am good only because I am alive and not because of the worthy things I do," you are likely to end up close to what we call the elegant therapeutic solution. That solution (like all things human, imperfectly stated and imperfectly executed by anyone) is to not rate your self or essence or personhood *at all*. Instead, you must learn to rate only what you think, feel, and *do*. You, of course, are responsible for your actions. But ideally you should rate only your *actions* and not your *youness* or *self*.

Learning not to rate yourself as a person means learning not to rate the personhood of others. Because this concept probably goes against the way most of you have been brought up, and it is possibly contrary to your biological nature, none of you is likely to become perfect at not judging others as persons any more than you are going to overcome the tendencies to rate your total selves. But if you become more conscious of how you are rating yourself and others, you can make a lot of progress—progress that will definitely help you in couplehood.

Is this all you have to know about REBT and how to get it all together for a happy and functional union? Not really! But it is not a bad beginning. What we've covered so far is not easy. It will take a lot of hard work on your part to successfully apply this chapter.

But this hard work will definitely pay off whether you are in or out of couplehood. Whether or not you take our advice is your choice, but if you take it, you may learn how to live more effectively and enjoyably. At the end of this chapter, you'll find a few exercises that will start you off on the hard—but very rewarding—work of achieving unconditional self-acceptance (USA) and other thoughts, feelings, and behaviors that will help you in your dating, relating, and mating goals.

EXERCISES TO KEEP YOU EMOTIONALLY FIT

It is easy to read about—and even to think about—what you're doing badly. We wrote this book to give you insight into how you and your mate are defeating yourselves and what you can do about changing. Insight, however, is not enough. Some of the most brilliant insights you have, and often keep having, can sound great. Utterly real. Quite convincing. But, as I, Dr. Ellis, discovered when I was a card-carrying psychoanalyst, some of these insights can be pretty useless.

One of my clients, a twenty-five-year-old teacher named Carol, who I saw in the 1950s, insisted that she had "good, healthy relations with her mother, father, and younger brother and couldn't understand why she was so hostile toward her boyfriend, Don. I soon found out that she was intensely jealous of her mother, terribly hurt by her father's favoring her brother, and exceptionally angry at her boyfriend for ignoring her demands for more affection. Carol was thrilled with these important insights and was sure that they explained her hostility. She thought that these revelations would cure her. Well, they didn't. For the next few months, Carol's rage against Don escalated and he threatened to break up with her. Carol was distraught about this—and about the dismal failure of her insights into her hidden feelings to help her.

Fortunately, I was becoming skeptical myself at that time about the virtues of psychoanalytic revelations. So I went back to the details of Carol's two-year relationship with Don, and soon helped her gain a different kind of insight. Carol had with Don—as she had had all her life with other relatives and friends—an overwhelming Irrational Belief. "I absolutely *need* significant people's approval. Without it, I am a thoroughly unlovable, worthless person!" While that shook Carol up, it still didn't quite change her.

REBT—which I was then formulating but hadn't quite developed—tries to help people with a number of non-psychoanalytic insights. Let's take a few moments to review these insights and how they relate to Carol's situation.

As we have already noted, people rarely just *get* emotionally upset. They also actively *make* themselves anxious, depressed, and hostile with their beliefs (Bs) *about* the unfortunate adversities (A's) that happen to them. So Carol was *believing*, "I absolutely *need* greater affection than Don usually expresses—or else I am a thoroughly unlovable, worthless person!" When she did not get—or *thought* she did not get—what she "needed" from Don, she felt worthless. Noting this feeling and believing that Don's neglect *made* her feel inadequate (which is a common belief of self-downing people), Carol defensively turned some of her self-hatred against Don. No matter when Carol started to believe her IB about direfully needing people's affection, she was still holding it *in the present*, though it seemed to have originated in her childhood and adolescence. But she *still* strongly believed it—both consciously and unconsciously. She could have originally held it and later given it up, which would have meant she would *no longer* have been affected by it at the time she was. But that was not the case.

So, with my help Carol began to have insights into her early *and* her remaining need for significant people's expression of affection. What she did not yet see—and what it took me another year to show her as I kept developing REBT—was that insight by itself is not enough. The only way to correct her hostility toward Don was through hard and persistent *work and practice*—yes, work, and yes, practice. She had to *change* her IBs. When she began to do that, she started to feel much less angry and much more loving toward Don.

Actually, as she gave up her dire *need* for Don's affection, she realized that he probably would never fulfill her *preference* for affection, so she *un*angrily broke up with him. Eventually she found another—more loving—partner, whom she eventually married.

This book looks at the principles and practices of REBT as they relate to dating, mating, and relating. But we also include a number of exercises for relevant homework. As Daniel Goleman and other psychologists have recently emphasized, humans have academic or intellectual intelligence, but they also have emotional and practical intelligence. In REBT terms, they can think, can think about their thinking, and think about thinking about their thinking. This enables them to observe, analyze, and change their IBs, their disturbed feelings, and their dysfunctional behaviors. REBT shows them how.

As a human, you have emotional intelligence—which includes self-awareness, self-control, persistence, self-motivation, and social deftness. As you can see, self-awareness includes a good deal of thinking and thinking about thinking—and so do the other aspects of emotional intelligence. But therapy requires a considerable amount of work and practice—of pushing yourself, pushing yourself, and pushing yourself. And it also involves a lot of time and effort when you're not "on the couch"—a lot of homework—to get results. If you want to use it to change yourself in the process and make yourself—yes, *make* yourself—less disturbed and more fulfilled, you had better do your homework.

Remember, you don't *have* to do your homework. You don't *have* to do anything. You don't *have* to change and you don't necessarily *have* to work in order to change. But you preferably should. Not for our sake, but for your own and for the sake of those you want to relate to intimately.

The exercises in this chapter are designed to put you in touch with your feelings. Your feelings keep you alive and happy, even your negative feelings. When something goes wrong in your life—some adversity (A), such as failure, rejection, or discomfort—you want to feel bad, not happy or neutral. If you lose a partner, a good job, or a tennis match, you can try to be optimistic and tell yourself,

"That's great! What a fine opportunity to learn from my mistakes! That gives me something to live for!" Which is fine. By all means, learn from your errors and don't beat yourself up. But watch it. What about acknowledging your healthy *bad* feelings, such as sorrow and regret? Such as frustration and annoyance? Such as real determination to do better in the future? These healthy negative feelings motivate you to look at your failings, to work at correcting them, and to push yourself to improve. They energize and expand you. They are not too pleasant—but they help.

REBT, though highly cognitive, stresses feelings: pleasurable feelings that add to your life and unpleasant feelings that *also* add to your life. But it doesn't look at *all* feelings. Not even all "high" feelings—like narcissism and grandiosity. While these have their place—in moderation—they can also sabotage you. For example, when you insist that you run the universe and therefore can get anything you want. You know where this leads you.

But worse than these feelings are your strong negative *unhealthy* feelings. You fail at love, work, or tennis and you choose to feel panicked, depressed, enraged. *Choose?* Yes, you have considerable choice here. Panic, depression, and rage won't get you very far. Will they get you more love, better work, greater wins at tennis? Hardly.

REBT, like other major therapies, deals with your feelings— good, bad, or indifferent. But it is unique, however, in that it helps you to distinguish between healthy and unhealthy negative feelings. When something goes wrong—or you *make* it wrong—in your partnership and in your life, it is healthy to feel *healthily* sorry, regretful, frustrated, and displeased. These feelings help you acknowledge, cope with, preferably change, or at worst accept adversities (A's) that you presently can't change. *Healthy* negative feelings can be aversive and unfriendly but they are not usually self-sabotaging.

Sample Exercise 1A: Becoming Aware of Your Healthy and Unhealthy Negative Feelings

List Some of My Main Goals, Purposes, and Values

My General Relating and Mating Goals

To find a suitable love partner.

To win his or her favor.

To build an ongoing relationship with him or her.

To maintain that steady relationship.

My Specific Goals

To discover more about my partner.

To see more of him or her.

To commit to him or her.

To have satisfactory sex with him or her.

To find enjoyable pursuits with him or her.

To discuss important questions with him or her.

To agree to differ at times with him or her.

To resolve some of my main disagreements with him or her.

To live successfully with my remaining disagreements with him or her.

To stop criticizing him or her.

To resolve my hostility toward him or her.

To get along well with my partner's parents.

To get along well with my partner's friends.

Exercise 1A

My General Relating and
Mating Goals
_____

Specific Relating and Mating
Goals
_____

_____   _____

_____   _____

_____   _____

_____   _____

_____   _____

_____   _____

_____   _____

_____   _____

_____   _____

_____   _____

_____   _____

_____   _____

Sample Exercise 1B: Becoming Aware of My Healthy and Unhealthy Negative Feelings When My Relating and Mating Goals Are Blocked and I Am Faced With Adversities (A's)

Adversities That Might Occur	Healthy Negative Feelings I Might Experience	Unhealthy Negative Feelings I Might Experience
I keep looking for but cannot find a suitable partner.	Disappointment	Depression; horror
I find a suitable partner but get rejected.	Sorrow; regret	Panic; depression
I get in a good relationship but it breaks up.	Real sadness; grief	Panic; depression; extreme loneliness
My partner disagrees with me on an important matter.	Disappointment; determination to reach an agreement	Anger; blaming my partner; panic
My partner severely criticizes me.	Keen disappointment; regret	Self-damning; rage at partner
My partner's mother is impossible.	Frustration; disappointment	Impatience; low frustration tolerance; anger at partner for making me visit his or her mother
My partner keeps avoiding me sexually.	Frustration; disappointment	Feelings of inadequacy; rage at partner; avoiding discussing this matter

Exercise 1B

Adversities That Might Occur	Healthy Negative Feelings I Might Experience	Unhealthy Negative Feelings I Might Experience

Sample Exercise 1C: What I Can Do to Change My Unhealthy Negative Feelings to Healthy Negative Feelings When I Am Faced with Relating and Mating Blocks and Adversities (A's)

Unhealthy Negative Feelings That I Might Experience	How I Can Change My Unhealthy Negative Feelings to Healthy Negative Feelings
Depression and horror when I cannot find a suitable partner.	I can transform my depression into keen disappointment by convincing myself that it is difficult but not impossible to find a suitable partner and that if I keep undepressively looking I will probably find one. I can accept the *bad* but not *awful* reality that if I never find a suitable partner I can still be a reasonably happy person.
Panic and depression when I find a suitable partner but then get rejected.	I can make myself feel only sorrow and regret by showing myself that I *can* find another suitable partner and succeed with him or her. I can convince myself that I may have failings for this potential mate but that I am not a *total failure*. I can show myself that rejection is *bad* but it is not *the end of the world*.
Panic, depression, extreme loneliness when I get in a good relationship but it breaks up.	I can make myself feel only real sadness and grief by convincing myself that being alone is very *uncomfortable* but not *horrible*; that it is most probably temporary and not permanent; and that perhaps I can learn from this break-up and later do better in a realationship with a partner more compatible with me.

Exercise 1C

Unhealthy Negative Feelings That I Actually Experience	How I Can Change My Unhealthy Negative Feelings to Healthy Negative Feelings
_____	_____
_____	_____
_____	_____
_____	_____
_____	_____
_____	_____
_____	_____
_____	_____
_____	_____
_____	_____
_____	_____
_____	_____
_____	_____
_____	_____
_____	_____
_____	_____
_____	_____
_____	_____

2

Getting Relationships Together as a Couple: Using the ABCs of REBT in Your Relationship

Marital problems, and the ABCs that lead to them, are usually more complicated than the problems of a single person, such as Charlene, trying to find a suitable mate. Take the case of Sid and Jo, a married couple who came to see me, Dr. Ellis, because, they said, they loved each other deeply but were incessantly fighting. Sid's initial ABCs were simple. He said that Jo gave him very little sex, but that she had the gall to lie and say that she often not only initiated but had sex with Sid. Let's chart Sid's ABCs, starting with the A's and the Cs:

Adversities: Jo had sex with Sid, he claimed, about once a month. Worse, she insisted that they really had sex at least once a week. Sid saw himself as being very sexually deprived, and Jo denied this.

Consequences: Sid was angry with Jo and insisted that she was a "goddamned liar." She fought back—and they both got nowhere.

Sid—as you might well guess—fully acknowledged his anger but insisted, "Jo keeps saying she loves me, but gives me very little sex. Then she lies about it and that makes me very angry!"

"Oh, no," I objected during my first session with this couple. "She can't make you angry. Only *you* can."

"Well, she does! So there!"

Let's assume that you are right about Jo's behavior. She gives you little sex and then insists that she gives you more than she actually does. These are the As in the ABCs of REBT, your adversities.

"They damned well are!"

Jo tried to interrupt at this point, to show that Sid was wrong, but I stopped her. I explained briefly to them that even if Sid was mistaken, he *still* was needlessly upsetting himself about it and I wanted to show him how wrong he was about his "rightness" about Jo's disturbing him. So she agreed and I continued, talking mainly to Sid.

"So Jo is presenting you with your A's—your adversities. But obviously she can't *make* you angry, which is your consequence."

"She damned well can—and does!"

"No. Because if a hundred Jos deprived a hundred Sids of sex—as let's assume your Jo is doing—would all the Sids be just as angry as you are? Think, now—would they?"

"*Most* of them would be!"

"Yes, they probably would. But *all* of them—the *whole* hundred?"

"Well, no. I guess not."

"How come? What would the few unangry Sids be doing, be saying to themselves, to stop from infuriating themselves about their Jo's rotten behavior?"

"Oh, I don't know. I guess something like, 'Too bad Jo is that way about sex, and about lying about it. But she has some other good traits, too. And I still love her for *those* traits.'"

"Good! See, you nicely figured it out. You figured out that the unangry Sids could tell themselves unangry, self-pacifying beliefs (Bs) about Jo and about the adversities (A's) she is creating for them. Fine! You very clearly showed that unfortunate A's, by themselves, do not create disturbed Cs like anger. It is your Bs, along with your As, that largely lead to disturbed Cs. Do you see that?"

Sid said reluctantly, "Well, yes. I guess so."

Great! I said to myself. *Half the battle won.*

Still talking mainly to Sid, but hoping that Jo was listening, I then tried to show him that his rage at his wife, his C, stemmed largely from two different types of beliefs (Bs). He initially had Irrational Beliefs (IBs): "Jo gives me very little sex—and then lies about it. Therefore, Jo doesn't love me." But eventually, by stepping back and thinking the situation through, he was able to develop healthy, Rational Beliefs (RBs): "I don't *like* Jo's depriving me of sex—and lying about it, no less! I *wish* she would treat me better! But if she doesn't, too bad. It's not the end of the world, and I can still live with her and enjoy her other good traits. But I still *wish* that she'd change and give me more sex."

If Sid had *only* had these RBs in the first place about his adversities, he would most probably—I tried to show him—have strong negative feelings about being deprived, such as healthy feelings of disappointment and frustration, but he would not have had unhealthy feelings of rage. In REBT, we call these Healthy Consequences (HCs). Why are they healthy? Because unlike Unhealthy Consequences (UCs), these might help Sid cope with his sex deprivation and, instead of fighting nastily with Jo about it, he might find a noncombative way to encourage her to have more sex with him.

Sid and I knew, however, that he was not merely disappointed and frustrated by Jo's sexual *behavior* but also enraged at *her* for acting this "terrible" way. I asked him if he could figure out the additional IBs that led to his rage, his consequence.

"Jo has *no right* to treat me so badly—and then, to boot, lie about *not* doing so!" he said. "She *shouldn't* be that unfair! How *terrible* she is. She's a nasty, lying, *rotten person!*"

Sid was right. Almost certainly, these were his main IBs. And typically, they included, first, a basic, underlying absolutistic *should* or *must:* "Jo *absolutely must not* act the way she is acting!" Second, going along with Sid's grandiose, dogmatic demand were his "logical" conclusions: "Because she is behaving in a sexually frustrating way as she *must not,* it is *terrible* (totally wrong and inconvenient) and she is a nasty, lying *rotten person* (incapable of practically ever acting considerately and lovingly)."

Let's take a few moments to look at the IBs of REBT. When I (Dr. Ellis) first developed REBT in the mid-1950s, and after using it for a while, I discovered several types of IBs. These included:

1. Absolutistic musts, shoulds, oughts, and demands, such as "I *must* perform all important tasks well!" and "I absolutely *have to be*

approved or loved by people I care for!" —also known as "musturbatory beliefs."

2. Core disturbing conclusions, which usually "logically" stem from or accompany these grandiose demands, such as, "If I don't do an important task well, as I absolutely must, I am an *incompetent, inadequate person!*" "If conditions are not as good for me as they *should* be and I get more frustrations than I *must* get, life is *awful* and *horrible* and I'll *never* be able to enjoy it at all!"

3. Automatic thoughts and unrealistic observations, which often stem from people's rigid musts and their core disturbing conclusions such as, "Because I absolutely *must* perform all important tasks well, and I will be an *incompetent, inadequate person* if I don't, I am sure that the paper I just wrote is one of the worst ever written and that I shall fail the course for which I wrote it" and "Because I *have to* win Jo's love and would be *totally unlovable* if I didn't, I am sure that I acted stupidly with her and that she will never have anything to do with me!"

What I came to learn through the years is that these beliefs are common, but that they work on different levels. The IBs of REBT changed and evolved throughout the next decades, basically demonstrating that people's—and couple's—absolutistic musts come first. At least, in the case of neurosis. I now assume—and most followers of REBT go along with me—that when you only have preferences and wishes, including *strong* preferences and wishes that you will tend to perform competently, that others will usually treat you nicely and fairly, and that the conditions under which you live will be good, you will rarely upset yourself when your preferences are not fulfilled. Yes, you will then rarely think, feel, and act neurotically.

However, when you strongly think and feel that you absolutely *must* perform well, *have to* be treated considerately by others, and utterly *need* your life conditions to be satisfactory, watch it—you're in trouble.

Once you consciously or unconsciously, explicitly or implicitly (tacitly) insist on any of the three basic musts—"*I* must perform well!" "*Others* must treat me nicely!" "*Conditions* must be comfortable and enjoyable!" —you then almost always create one or more accompanying core IBs that appreciably add to your insistent musts. These include:

1. *Awfulizing.* "Because *I* didn't do as well as I *must*, it's *awful* (just about as bad as it can be)!" "Because *you* don't treat me as nicely as you *absolutely should*, it's *terrible* (totally bad)!" and "Because the *conditions* under which I live are not as good as they ought to be, it's *horrible* (thoroughly unlivable)!"

2. *I can't-stand-it-itis.* "Because I did poorly, or you *treated me* poorly, or conditions dealt with me poorly—none of which *must* exist—I *can't stand* it, *can't bear* it (can't be happy *at all*)!"

3. *Damnation.* "Because I keep failing at important things, just as I *must* not, I'm *no good* and *don't deserve* a decent life!" and "Because you don't treat me as well as you *should*, you're a *rotten, damnable* person!"

4. *Allness and neverness.* "Because I failed to win your love, as I absolutely *must*, I'll *never* win the love of a worthy person!" and "Because you failed to treat me properly, as you *invariably must*, you'll *always* behave poorly and *never* be lovable!"

Over the course of our sessions, I helped Sid to see that Jo may well have been depriving him of "good sex" —his adversity (A) — and perhaps also had been exaggerating or lying about how much sex they were regularly having. But he was largely *making* himself enraged at her—his consequence (C) —by insisting, because of his belief system (B), that she absolutely *should not, must not* act the way she presumably *was* acting. So it was not his *preferences* at B ("I *wish* Jo would give me more regular sex") but his grandiose *demand* at B ("She therefore *must* give me the sex that I prefer!") that was largely creating his rage at Jo, his consequence (C).

Sid's admission that he was largely upsetting himself was great. So I briefly showed him that his self-disturbing beliefs could in fact be disputed (D) and changed back to healthy preferences. When he questioned and challenged his IBs, he came up with these disputes and answers:

Dispute: "Why has Jo *no right* to treat me so badly and then lie about doing so?"

Answer: "She has every right, as a fallible human, to do whatever she does—including depriving me sexually and then refusing to admit her poor behavior. Like all humans, she has the right to be wrong—even to me!"

Dispute: "Where is it written that Jo *shouldn't* be as unfair as she is to me?"

Answer: "It is not written anywhere—except in my head. She *should* be unfair right now—because she is that way at present. If she is really acting unfairly—as I am sure that she is—she *has* to act that way. How can she be fair when she's actually unfair. No way!"

Dispute: "Is it really *terrible* that Jo is treating me unfairly?"

Answer: "No—it's very bad and, to me, very inconvenient. But not *totally* bad. It could be worse—much worse. She could deprive me sexually *and* rob me, hurt me, even kill me."

Dispute: "How does her rotten behavior, if I see it correctly, make her a *nasty, lying, rotten person?*"

Answer: "It doesn't. She doesn't *always* act nastily, lyingly, and rottenly, as a thoroughly *rotten person* would. Even when she acts damnably she is not a subhuman, damnable *person*. She often *does* badly but she *is not* her bad behavior because she also does many good and neutral things. So I can legitimately deplore some of the things she does but not blame her *entire personhood* for doing these things."

I helped Sid with this disputing and answering and also, as I usually do, got Jo into the act. She came up with the idea that if she *always* did bad things to Sid and everyone else she would still not be a thoroughly *rotten person* because she might change and do neutral or good deeds in the future. Her point helped both of them to see that there are really no *good people* nor *bad people* but just people who *up to now* have done a number of bad acts but who might well change in the future.

As Jo put it, "I am a *process*, not a *thing*, and as a process I can always change."

"Yes," Sid jokingly added. "And you may even become too sexy for me and insist that I have much *more* sex than we are now having."

"Fat chance!" said Jo, and we all laughed.

I spent about twenty minutes of their first marital counseling session helping Sid to see that no matter how wrong and unfair Jo might be about depriving him sexually, his anger at her for doing so was largely self-created and could soon be uncreated. He agreed and Jo was particularly pleased with this part of our session. For she felt less threatened when we were talking about *Sid's* emotional problems, had little resistance to seeing how *he* largely created them, and could at least vaguely see that most of the points I was making about him could well apply to her. She began to recognize, while we were talking about Sid, that she was upsetting herself, too.

Jo's main problem—her disturbed consequence (C)—was depression mixed with guilt. Her main adversity was Sid's rage at her (his C). Her RBs were: "I hate Sid's being enraged at me. What a drag! Especially when I'm doing my best to satisfy him sexually." These RBs led to her healthy consequences (HC), feelings of disappointment and frustration.

Jo's IBs, which I quickly helped her see, especially since she had already learned some of the ABCs of REBT by listening to and participating in solving Sid's problem of anger, were: "I *absolutely must not* be angrily criticized by Sid! I *have to* please him sexually and am not doing what I have to do! How awful! He's right about my failing him and that makes me a hopeless failure!" As a consequence (C) of these IBs, Jo felt guilty and depressed.

As I did with Sid, I helped Jo to actively and forcefully dispute (D) her IBs and to show herself that: (1) there was no reason she *absolutely must not* be angrily criticized by Sid, (2) she didn't *have to* please him sexually, though that would be *preferable*, and (3) she may well have been failing Sid sexually but that didn't make her a failure. When she started to see this, she felt keenly disappointed with some of her behaviors—especially her lying to Sid that they were having more sex than they actually were having. But she was only guilty about her actions or inactions and no longer put herself down for behaving this way. She therefore lost most of her depression.

I am, however, getting ahead of my story, because I really want to show, in this chapter, how complicated some of the disturbances in marriage are; and how they interact with the other partner's upsetnesses.

It took us several sessions to figure out the following interrelationships between Sid's and Jo's disturbance; but when we did so they were most illuminating to both of them. They also showed how these kinds of problems frequently arise in marriage and lead to more and more problems.

Partners are often affected by the dysfunctional Cs (consequences) of the other partner. If Sid makes himself angry at Jo, she may easily make herself guilty about "causing" his anger. If Sid makes himself very critical of Jo, she may easily make herself very self-downing about "making" him critical. Similarly, if Jo makes herself angry at Sid, he may easily use her anger as an A (activizing event or adversity) and make himself angry at her—or he may blame himself for "creating" her anger. Each partner frequently disturbs himself or herself about the other partner's disturbed reactions.

Fortunately, however, one partner's disturbed emotions and actions importantly *contribute to*, but do not actually *make*, the other partner "crazy." Consequently, if either or both of them learn and use the ABCs of human disturbance that are described in REBT, they can, after a while, undisturb themselves about the other's disturbance. After even a longer period of time, they can get so good at doing this that either or both of them may become much less disturb*able*, and may refuse to overreact to the other's overreactions.

This is what happened, at first, in Jo's case. Though she had a long history of making herself neurotic about her relationships and about other adversities in her life, and though at first she was much more disturbed—depressed—than Sid, she soon started to do two things: She acknowledged that she, and not only Sid, made herself upset about the unfortunate things that happened in their marriage;

and, second, she saw that Sid had many self-disturbing tendencies, too—that he made himself needlessly upset about her "poor" behaviors and that she also unduly disturbed herself about his upsetness. When she worked on these problems—including somewhat similar ones that she experienced in her work as a teacher—she began to give herself unconditional acceptance, to give Sid unconditional acceptance as well, and to accept some rotten conditions—especially those in the school system in which she worked—without wailing and whining about them.

After eight sessions of REBT with her husband, Jo was confronted with the grim reality that Sid's parents, who had always hated her taking their darling boy away from them, had put up considerable money—which they could really not afford—to help Sid's sister and her husband buy a fairly luxurious home, while refusing to help Sid and her out in any way when they wanted to borrow a modest sum to make a down payment on their own new home. Normally, Jo would have made herself exceptionally angry at Sid's parents for being so unfair, as well as depressed about the fact that they did not sufficiently care for her and probably thought that she was a "worthless person" who didn't deserve to live in a reasonably nice home while her brother-in-law and sister-in-law were "good people" who deserved the very best kind of home. She would have worked on these feelings of anger and depression, ultimately forgiven Sid's father and mother, and gone on with her life.

This time, however, she only felt moderately disappointed with what had happened. She used REBT to combat her feelings of anger and depression in regard to Sid, and was successful in doing this on several occasions. So when she learned about her in-laws' "crummy" and "unfair" actions, she almost automatically said to herself, "Look, what's the use of upsetting myself about this? They always did act this way to me—probably because I took their 'nice' boy away from them. No matter. That's their nature, and they are merely showing it once again. I wish to hell they weren't that way; but damn it, they are! Tough! Sid and I will just have to find some other way to get a sizable down payment on the home that we really want, and luckily we won't be beholden to them for helping us get it. It means nothing about me or about Sid—just about them. Too bad!"

So Jo's use of REBT really paid off. Her marriage with Sid improved remarkably, including her willingness to satisfy him sexually even when she didn't feel particularly sexy herself. And just as his Cs had sparked her IBs and UCs, her RBs and HCs now encouraged healthy reactions in her husband when unfortunate adversities occurred. Their bickering largely ceased and they enjoyed being together much more than they had before they began to understand and to use the ABCs of REBT.

EXERCISES FOR CHAPTER TWO

In this chapter, we showed how Jo and Sid discovered, acknowledged, and worked to dispute some of their main IBs—particularly their self-defeating demands that led to their feelings of anger at each other and guilt about their own feelings and behaviors. Now let's do some exercises that will help you disclose your own dating, relating, and mating irrationalities, show you how to dispute them and come up with effective new philosophies.

Sample Exercise 2A: List of the Main Unfortunate Activating Events of Adversities (A's) in My Life—Particularly Those About My Dating, Relating, and Mating Problems—And My Main Unhealthy Feelings and Behaviors That Accompany Them

Unfortunate Activating Events or Adversities Now In My Life	Unhealthy Feelings and Behaviors That Often Accompany These Events
Not being able to find a suitable partner.	Depression. Horror. Withdrawing and giving up on looking. Foolishly continuing with unsuitable partner.
Getting rejected by a suitable partner.	Panic. Depression. Refusing to date or to get involved again.
Recent breakup of a previously good relationship.	Depression. Severe anxiety. Compulsively seeking a new partner. Settling for an unsuitable partner.
Present partner disagrees with me on important matters. Present partner is very critical of me.	Anger at him or her. Criticizing him or her severely. Putting myself down severely. Becoming very defensive and not acknowledging my failings. Hating my partner.
Present partner is sexually unresponsive to me.	Feeling very inadequate. Plaguing my partner for more sex. Avoiding discussing reasons for partner's avoidance.

Exercise 2A

Unfortunate Activating Events or Adversities in My Life	Unhealthy Feelings and Behaviors That Often Accompany These Adversities

Sample Exercise 2B: List of Dysfunctional or Irrational Beliefs (IBs) That I Create to Produce My Unhealthy Dating, Relating, and Mating Feelings and Behaviors (Cs) That Accompany My Adversities (A's)

Unhealthy Feelings and Behaviors	My Irrational Beliefs Creating These Unhealthy Feelings and Behaviors
Depression and withdrawal at not finding a suitable partner.	I *must* find a suitable partner or else I'm no good! I'm unable to find a suitable partner! What's the use of looking. I'd better give up!
Panic and depression after getting rejected by a suitable partner. Withdrawal.	*I* absolutely must not get rejected—or else I'm no good! No suitable person will ever accept me! I'd better become a monk or a nun!
Depression and anxiety and settling for an unsuitable partner when a previously good relationship breaks up.	I *can't* maintain a good relationship! It's *too hard* to find a suitable partner! It *must not* be that hard!
Anger at partner for "unfair" criticism. Severely criticizing partner in return.	He or she *must not* criticize me unfairly after all I do for him or her! I'll show him or her how bad s/he really is!
Anger at partner for disagreeing on an important matter. Very critical of partner.	Since I'm right about this matter, s/he *absolutely must* go along with me. How stupid s/he is for disagreeing like this!
Self-downing when partner is sexually avoidant. Avoiding discussing reasons for partner's avoidance but keep plaguing my partner for more sex.	I must be sexually repulsive if my my partner avoids me. S/he *should* explain why s/he keeps avoiding me. S/he *must* try to satisfy me.

Exercise 2B

Unhealthy Feelings and Behaviors (Cs) That I Actually Experience	Irrational Beliefs (IB's) That I Create to Produce My Unhealthy Feelings and Behaviors (Cs)
_____	_____
_____	_____
_____	_____
_____	_____
_____	_____
_____	_____
_____	_____
_____	_____
_____	_____
_____	_____
_____	_____
_____	_____
_____	_____
_____	_____

Sample Exercise 2C: Ways of Disputing the Irrational Beliefs (IBs) That I Create to Produce My Unhealthy Dating, Relating, and Mating Feelings and Behaviors (Cs) That Accompany My Adversities (A's)

My Irrational Beliefs (IBs) About Relating and Mating	Disputing My IBs	Rational Answers to My Disputing
I *must* find a suitable partner or else I'm no good!	Why *must* I find a suitable partner, no matter how preferable it might be? How does failing to find one make *me* a failure for being alone?	I don't *have to* find what would be preferable. Failing at finding a partner never makes *me* a total failure.
I *must not* get rejected after first finding a suitable partner! If I do, I'll *never* be able to keep one!	What is the evidence that I *must* never get rejected and can *never* keep a suitable partner?	Only in my nutty head! I may find it *difficult* but not *impossible* to keep a suitable partner.
I *can't* maintain a good relationship. It *must not* be that hard—and it's *awful* that it is!	Prove that I *can't* maintain a good relationship. Why must it not be so hard to do so? How is it *awful* that it is hard to find a suitable partner?	I can only prove that I haven't *yet* maintained a good relationship, not that I *can't*. It must be hard to find one if it *is* hard—and that's highly inconvenient but not *awful*.
My partner *must* not criticize me unfairly! That proves how wholly rotten he or she is.	Where is it written that my partner *must* not criticize me unfairly? How does his or her rotten *behavior* make him or her wholly rotten?	It's not written anywhere that he or she has the right to criticize me unfairly. If my partner is *acting* badly, he or she is obviously not a wholly *rotten person.*

Sample Exercise 2C (cont.)

My Irrational Beliefs (IBs) About Relating and Mating	Disputing My IBs	Rational Answers to My Disputing My IBs
Since I'm right about this important matter with which I disagree with my partner, he or she *absolutely must* go along with me. He or she is an idiot for contradicting me! I must be sexually repulsive if my partner avoids me. He or she *should* explain why and *must* try to satisfy me!	Am I completely right about this matter? Even if I am, *must* my partner absolutely go along with me? If he or she doesn't, how does that make him or her an idiot? How does my partner's avoiding me sexually show that I am a repulsive person? Does my partner *have to* explain his or her avoiding and *have to* satisfy me sexually?	Even if I am right—and I obviously may *not* be—he or she *can* easily disagree with me. This may be quite wrong but never makes him or her a *total* idiot. My partner may avoid me sexually for many different reasons. Even if she or he finds me repulsive this doesn't prove that I am repulsive to *everyone*. He or she clearly doesn't *have to* explain the avoidance or satisfy me sexually, though that would be great!

Exercise 2C

My Irrational Beliefs (IBs) About Relating and Mating	Disputing My IBs	Rational Answers to My Disputing My IBs
_____	_____	_____
_____	_____	_____
_____	_____	_____
_____	_____	_____
_____	_____	_____
_____	_____	_____
_____	_____	_____
_____	_____	_____
_____	_____	_____
_____	_____	_____
_____	_____	_____
_____	_____	_____
_____	_____	_____
_____	_____	_____
_____	_____	_____
_____	_____	_____

3

Starting Out With Realistic Views of Couplehood

In reading the preface, you learned that in this book we are using the term "intimacy" to refer to any close relationship between two people. Although we certainly intend to analyze the erotic component of intimacy (which is present in many close relationships), we are not limiting intimacy to sex. We are likewise not contending that intimacy cannot be achieved by more than two people. Most people seem to develop close personal relationships as couples and our focus is to help them to do so in more satisfying ways.

The first session that I (Dr. Harper) had with Heather and George several years ago brings out some things to keep in mind as you explore potential couplehood. Heather was twenty, and George was twenty-one.

Heather: We're planning to live together, and we thought it was a good idea to talk to an expert about it. I suppose I should say *I* thought so because I'm afraid George still thinks it is a *dumb* idea.

George: Not stupid—just unnecessary. We haven't even lived together yet. So how can we discuss our problems sensibly with a counselor until we have experienced them? They may or may not be problems we can solve ourselves. If we can't, *then* it may be advisable to see a counselor.

Heather: Oh, George, you're not being honest. Last night you said that these counselor characters take huge fees to tell people what they already know or what they will find useless to learn.

George: It's true I've heard such comments from others and am inclined to believe them. But I am here, so why is it still a problem?

R.A.H.: Actually, you are both right. Heather is wise in wanting to prepare for and reduce problems you may encounter in living together and in believing that someone who has specialized in work with couples might be helpful. George is right, on the other hand, in seeing that a lot of pap is dished out in one form or another in this and other areas of psychotherapy. I think my pap-dishing is minimal, but that's up to you to decide as we go along.

Just on the basis of what you've already said, I'd like to make several points. First of all, it is evident that you already have a close personal relationship, so George's wait-and-see attitude doesn't entirely fit reality. Living together may well bring additional joys and woes, but much of the pattern of your intimacy has been already set (not set in concrete, we hope, for it is our job to de-set or un-set or even upset some of the patterns that are causing problems or that look as if they could lead to future difficulties). Second, you already have problems as a couple. It's probably safe to say that all couples (and persons, for that matter) have problems. The question is, "What are *our* problems and how can we effectively deal with them?" One problem that you demonstrated splendidly at the outset is that you are relatively inexperienced as personal problem solvers. From what you have said so far, though, I believe that an important difference in your approaches to problem-solving is that Heather seems willing to subject herself to a counseling experience that has a good chance of improving her skills in this area, while George seems more reluctant to do so.

George: I'm here. What's the problem?

R.A.H.: Yes, you are here, and for us to try to deal with couple-hood, your presence is desirable and perhaps essential. I was not giving you a hard time, but rather I wanted to point out that reluctance to look at a situation objectively in the presence of an experienced and trained third party tends to block the thinking or problem-solving process. Would you be willing to explore with

Heather and me some of the things you think may be leading you to be reluctant?

George: Well, I'm not sure. You say your fees are not so high, but they are high for Heather and me. And all I've heard from you so far sounds very theoretical. In fact, it sounds like bullshit.

R.A.H.: Bullshit it may well be. On the other hand, it may seem theoretical to you because you may be denying the existence of problems in your and Heather's relationship. If that's the case, trying to do something about problems you deny the existence of can seem intellectual or theoretical rather than realistic, personal, practical, and gutsy. I once saw a war casualty in a veterans' hospital who denied that he had lost a leg. Therefore (until we had overcome some of the denial, and he began to look at the reality of a missing leg), anything I asked him or suggested to him about adjusting to life as a person with just one leg was too nauseatingly theoretical to him.

Now your denial, George, is not so deep, complete, and intense as the veteran's. Otherwise I believe you would have refused to come here even once. If you are avoidant we can have trouble in looking at and doing something about things that Heather or I see as problems. Believe me, we will not always see things similarly, nor will I "side" with Heather. In fact, I am only on Heather's "side" now in the sense that I believe couples generally have problems, and you two in your brief interactions here have, in my opinion, already manifested some. My allegedly theoretical efforts so far have been directed toward seeing if we can begin looking and working at some of your interactional difficulties and improve your skills in the process.

George: Yeah, well, while I still think you talk too much and too theoretically, I am willing to buy into the idea that Heather and I need to improve our problem-solving skills and that *in case* we get problems we may become top-ho problem-solvers. Beyond that I won't go.

George at this point smiled at both Heather and me, and Heather walked over to George's chair to kiss him and tell him he was marvelously flexible and the light of her life and so forth. This was an excellent development—George's deciding he wanted to become a better problem-solver and Heather's immediately rewarding him, whether or not this was what she intended for changing, or at least relaxing, his problem-denial and indicating a desire to learn. Not only was the couple better able to look at and try to do something about their difficulties, they also had more positive feelings toward each other and toward undertaking problem-solving.

Neither luck nor magic, of course, provides the best explanation of how and why George and Heather got to a point where they could begin to learn to relate more effectively. As with any other kind of negotiation (labor-management, nation-to-nation, or whatever), couples need to develop means of negotiating ways of opening honest (but not devastating) interchanges. This helps them discern problems to discuss.

What are some of the important points in this interview with Heather and George? How can you use them in your own coupling effort? Let us break them down.

Nondefensiveness

People generally tend to dig in and hold fast to whatever point of view they have (often unthinkingly) arrived at—especially in those views involved with their sense of selfhood, for this influences most of their behavior. Thus, George had his sense of self-worth attached to the propositions that: (1) he (and he and Heather as a couple) had no problems, and (2) that *he* (not some fuzzy-headed counselor) would beautifully deal with any problems he and Heather would have living together. His *grandiosity* was at work.

Direct and immediate attack of George's defense of denial might, of course, strengthen it. Because we try to live by and not just promulgate REBT, I didn't tie in my own sense of self-worth with my profession. I tried to help George (and Heather) by interacting nondefensively with him, including returning geniality for persistent put-downs. This enabled George to reconsider his denial. He could even relax a little, and later "buy" my problem-solving proposition. Just as important, I provided a model of nondefensiveness for both Heather and George to start (perhaps unconsciously) to apply to their own interactions.

It is highly desirable for a therapist to contribute to the reduction of defensiveness. While couplehood has no copyright on defensiveness, close relationships tend to bring out and exaggerate many destructive tie-ins of behavior with self-esteem.

We shall say a lot more about the desirability of couples' developing nondefensiveness and about the importance of learning not to rate your *self* or *personhood,* but only rating yours and other people's *behavior,* because engagement in the personhood-rating process is deeply ingrained and is often enormously pernicious in human relationships.

Authenticity of the Therapist

Therapists are frequently taught to be "authentic" and to be "genuinely themselves" (whatever that might mean). We want to stress the importance of my congruent behavior (thoughts, feelings, perceptions, and actions) in my relating to Heather and George. I could hardly teach and model desirable interacting for them if my own thoughts, feelings, perceptions, and actions kept galloping off in different directions. For example, if I tagged myself a guru (personhood-rating), I would then believe I was deserving of deference, which would likely cause me to perceive George as a dreadful young upstart (more personhood rating) for calling my fine and beautiful wisdom "bullshit." If I were too egocentric, no matter how hard I tried to control my expression of feelings or my tone of voice, I might have come through to both George and Heather as a phony (although they might not have been immediately aware that they were reacting to me that way). Since close personal relationships demand reliability, and since problem-solving is sabotaged when phony thoughts, feelings, and actions infect the boiling pot of problems, the therapist's authenticity is important to communicate to a couple to help them enhance their own relationship.

Antiperfectionism

Perfectionism is one of the great scourges of human existence, especially in trying to effect an enjoyable relationship. Ironically, parents, teachers, and other influential people (including, alas, some therapists) tend to extol perfectionistic strivings in the young and impressionable. ["It brings out the best in us," the saying goes, "to keep striving for high and even unattainable goals and to be dissatisfied with anything less."]

Quite the contrary. Children quickly learn that it is impossible to meet adult ideals ("Why don't you get all A's?"), so they make various adaptations. One is to deny their failure to meet rigid standards; another is to avoid activities where perfect standards are demanded. (Perfectionists tend to consider only "important" goals toward which to strive, but their inconsistency is common.) Still another reaction is to internalize the perfectionist expectations and to judge your *self* an unsatisfactory human being when you (inevitably) fail to achieve ideal *performance*. (Remember Charlene in chapter one, who thought she was a shit because she was not rolling along ideally toward heterosexual heaven?) You believe that if you are not perfect in whatever you design as *the important* aspects of life, you're an indubitable turd. All your efforts either to deny your imperfection or to deny the *importance* of your undeniable failings are futile in the long run because you still subscribe to the deeply instilled belief that it is terrible not to be perfect, and if you do not function ideally, you are no good.

When perfectionism is carried into a close personal relationship, you not only continue to experience your own difficulties, you also often extend them to your partner and to the relationship itself. This *must* measure up to impossible ideals. Whether you are in a business or personal partnership, you demand that it must be the best because you deem it very important. "I, am no damned good if any of my important relationships are not the best! I, therefore, *must* guarantee that I, my partner, and our relationship all function ideally—or at least *seem* to function ideally." As a perfectionist, you often are unable to hide "horrible" imperfections from yourself, and you may try to hide them from others and consider yourself even more reprehensible for your concealing efforts. If you tie in with another perfectionist, difficulties may (or may not) multiply. We have rarely seen a couple where each person's idealistic rigidities gear with the other's and help them both to function satisfactorily.

Let's get back to Heather and George. George's denial that there were any important problems that could not be readily handled stemmed from his perfectionist perception of himself and of extensions of himself (Heather and the relationship). If he admitted to the possibility of problems—and especially to the need for help in facing and dealing with them—then the idea of a-okay George was all shot to hell, with nothing but George the nebbish left. This thinking in extremes is characteristic of perfectionists. If, for example, they put a lot of importance on grades in school, then an A-minus or a B-plus is the same as a failing grade. It was a first-step victory in the long, hard road of overcoming perfectionism for George to agree to try to learn how to improve his problem-solving skills. He could do this within the favorable ambiance of the therapy session because he was not having his defense of denial directly attacked. He was being asked simply to participate in a (to him) theoretical process of enhancing his problem-solving skills in his relationship with Heather. Since we began to get into some problems even in our first session and since George was by no means stupid, he began (he later admitted) to let some of his denial melt away.

Heather was a somewhat different story. Because I found it desirable to focus at first on George's situation, there was danger that Heather might begin to think she was an innocent and virtuous bystander. While it turned out that she had some disturbed tendencies (many of us do), she was committed to facing and trying to work out difficulties in herself and in the relationship with George. Even such a commitment, however, may itself sometimes conceal perfectionistic tendencies that need to be examined. Namely: "If George and I (Heather) work hard and do all the things the therapist says, then we'll have no more problems and will live happily every after. After we get this magic overhaul job, we will achieve perfection."

No. A close personal relationship does not necessarily become fascinating and enjoyable when problems disappear. Problems may improve, but problems also remain. Couples who learn effectively and steadily to *cope* with problems will likely find fuller satisfaction.

EXERCISES FOR CHAPTER 3

Couplehood has many joys and disadvantages, just like any other type of relationship. Some of the main troubles with mating, particularly in a culture like our own where romantic ideals of love and marriage are prominent, are the unrealistic expectations with which two partners often get together. Disillusionment follows from illusion. As REBT notes, the road to hell is frequently paved with exaggerated or false expectations. It is not merely the hassles of mating—adversities (A's)—that lead to separation and divorce—consequences (Cs)—but the utopian and perfectionistic beliefs (Bs) about the difficulties of successful mating.

What are some of the unrealistic and illogical beliefs that you—like millions of other partners—may bring to your partnership? And what are some of the realistic, rational beliefs with which you could replace them? Let us complete this exercise by listing some of the main IBs that you may imbibe from your culture and concoct yourself that may disrupt your relationships, and then substituting some of the realistic RBs with which you could replace them.

Exercise 3A: Some Common Unrealistic and Irrational Beliefs (IBs) and Expectations That I May Hold About Mating

Circle whether you hold the following beliefs: S (Strongly), M (Moderately Strongly), or W (Weakly).

			Some Common Unrealistic and Irrational Beliefs (IBs) and Expectations That I May Hold About Mating
S	M	W	Because my partner and I really love each other, we will rarely strongly disagree with each other.
S	M	W	When my partner and I strongly disagree with each other, we will always talk out our disagreements and work hard at making compromises.
S	M	W	I can expect my partner to practically always satisfy me sexually when I desire satisfaction even if s/he is not in the mood to have sex at that time.
S	M	W	Because I generally love my partner, I will be madly in love and be excited to be with him or her at practically all times.
S	M	W	Because my partner generally loves me, s/he will be madly in love and excited to be with me at practically all times.
S	M	W	Being with my partner means having some problems but will also mean having so many pleasures and advantages that I will practically never upset myself about the difficulties of mating and will never really think about separating from him or her.
S	M	W	Because I really love my partner, I will never think of being strongly attracted to someone else, nor think about having love or sex relations with another person.
S	M	W	If my partner and I have children together, I shall only love and cherish them and never be out of sorts with and angry at them.

Some Common Unrealistic and Irrational Beliefs (IBs) and Expectations That I May Hold
About Mating

S   M   W   If my partner and I have children together, we
shall put their interests first and never fight with
each other to get them to do the "right" things.

S   M   W   I shall always cooperate with my mate's relationship with his or her family and try never to
make myself angry at him or her nor at his or
her family members.

S   M   W   Other unrealistic IBs that I hold about mating
(specify):_____

_____

_____

_____

_____

_____

_____

_____

Exercise 3B: Some Realistic and Rational Beliefs (RBs) and Expectations That I Will Try to Hold and Maintain About Mating

Circle whether you will work at holding the following rational beliefs: S (Strongly), M (Moderately Strongly), or W (Weakly).

			Realistic and Rational Beliefs (RBs) and Expectations I Will Work at Holding and Maintaining
S	M	W	Even though my partner and I really love each other, we can easily strongly disagree with one another.
S	M	W	When my partner and I strongly disagree with each other, we may easily and often slip, make ourselves angry, fail to talk about our disagreements, and therefore fail to work at making effective compromises.
S	M	W	I should not unrealistically expect my partner to always want to have sexual relations with me when I really want to have them.
S	M	W	I should not unrealistically expect my partner to satisfy me sexually even when s/he is not in the mood for sex.
S	M	W	Even though I generally love my partner, I will realistically expect that I will not be madly in love nor excited to be with him or her at practically all times.
S	M	W	Even though my partner generally loves me, I will not realistically expect that s/he will be madly in love nor excited to be with me at practically all times.
S	M	W	Even though I generally love my partner, I will realistically expect myself to be inconsiderate and selfish to him or her at times.

Exercise 3B (cont.)

Realistic and Rational Beliefs (RBs) and
Expectations I Will Work at Holding and
Maintaining

S   M   W   Even though my partner generally loves me, I
will realistically expect him or her to be inconsiderate and selfish to me at times.

S   M   W   Even though being with my partner has many
pleasures and advantages, I will realistically expect that sometimes I will upset myself about
the difficulties of mating and may sometimes
even think of separating from him or her.

S   M   W   Even though I really love my partner, I will realistically expect to be strongly attracted to someone else and to think about having love or sexual
relations with him or her.

S   M   W   If my partner and I have children together, I will
realistically expect that I will be out of sorts and
angry at them even though I love them.

S   M   W   If my partner and I have children together, I will
realistically expect that we will sometimes put
our own interests first and fight with each other
to get the children to do what s/he or I feel are
the "right" things.

S   M   W   I will realistically expect that I will not always
cooperate with his or her relationship with his
or her family and will sometimes make myself
angry at his or her family members.

S   M   W   Other realistic and rational beliefs (RBs) I will
work at having and maintaining in my mating
relationship (specify): _____

_____

_____

We shall now give Exercise 3C, REBT's Famous Shame-Attacking Exercise and other emotional-evocative exercises. But first, let us say more about unconditional self-acceptance (USA) which these exercises address.

Psychotherapists—and philosophers before them—have struggled for years to find and cure the one central or core problem of disturbed people. Why? Partly because humans like to simplify complex things—and to figure out one crucial, and presumably final, answer to the difficult human condition. We probably never will find this core problem, because humans *are* complex—and so are their woes.

Of the many existent therapies, REBT is one of the simplest and tightest. It says that practically all people's neuroses—not their severe personality disorders and their psychoses—involve or are largely sparked by their absolutistic shoulds, oughts, musts, and demands. And REBT has an excellent record of helping tens of thousands of clients, as well as millions of readers, to see their musturbatory thinking, feeling, and behaving, to change it to strong preferring, and—voila!—to significantly improve.

But REBT also includes many related, more complex theories. For example: (1) Musts and demands are not *merely* cognitive but *also* emotional *and* behavioral, (2) they are not *merely* learned or innately created but *also* imbibed, practiced, *and* manufactured, (3) they are not *only* experienced and followed in childhood and adolescence but *also* reconditioned and actively reconstructed in the present, (4) they are not *simply* changed to helpful preferences by people's making a profound philosophical change but *also* modified by their using a large number of cognitive, emotive, and behavioral exercises and techniques, (5) people's absolutistic and dogmatic thinking and experiences are quite individualistic and self-destructive but *also* stem from cultural and subcultural teachings and can be harmful, and (6) human goals, purposes, experiences, and personality are again personal and individual but are *also* amazingly social and cultural.

So REBT is simple—and has its complications. It is constructivist and postmodern—and also (hopefully) scientific, practical, and efficient. Read Ellis's revised and updated edition of *Reason and Emotion in Psychotherapy* and see for yourself.

Back to self-help basics. REBT theorizes that you tend to have two major IBs when you think, feel, and act self-defeatingly: (1) self-deprecation, self-downing, or self-damning—"I *absolutely must* perform well and be approved by significant others or else *I* am, my *person* is, incompetent and worthless!" and (2) low frustration tolerance (LFT) or discomfort, anxiety, rage, and depression—"Conditions and other people *absolutely must be* easy, comfortable, and enjoyable, and *absolutely must not be* very frustrating and depriving, or else people and/or the world are no damned good. I *can't stand* it, and my life is *awful!*" These two IBs often interact, reinforce, and complicate each other and lead to mental and physical "horror" and pain. Moreover, when they help to create physical and emotional disturbance, we humans—including you—often have self-downing and low frustration tolerance *about* our disturbances. Result: more disturbance.

In this chapter we looked at Heather's and George's defensiveness, lack of authenticity, and perfectionism. But aren't these disturbances all related to self-downing? Intimately! In some ways they are products of, or what in REBT we actually call *derivatives* of self-deprecation. For if Heather and George and the rest of the human race were not self-downers, how would they ever be defensive, inauthentic, or perfectionistic? Not very easily.

When you are defensive—that is, when you deny your failings to yourself and others and fail to *be* "yourself"—you are scared that they will witness your flaws and (of course) down you for having them. You are *afraid of* severe criticism. So defensiveness, when you could be honest and perhaps be severely penalized, in large part *is* highly *conditional* self-acceptance instead of *unconditional* self-acceptance.

Isn't lack of authenticity pretty similar? Indeed so. When you are inauthentic you pose, pretend, posture, and put on an act. Again, you *refuse* to be "yourself," because if you were, other people would presumably down your "real" self—would down *you*. More important, you would *agree* with them that you *are* no good.

Perfectionism is in the same class—piled higher and deeper. Following it, you believe that you have to do *perfectly* well at important tasks—and be *perfectly* approved by significant others. And if not, back to self-downing you go. Other people witness your imperfections and supposedly put *you*, the person, down. And again, you fully agree.

All of the above illustrates what we touched on in chapter one. Unless you decide to commit to and work hard at achieving *un*conditional self-acceptance, you will cultivate self-downing—and be a willing victim of your partner's and other people's assaults on your personhood. Moreover, when your partner inevitably exhibits flaws and unniceties, will you really resist denigrating him or her? Not very likely.

So, how can you powerfully, consistently, and persistently avoid the pitfalls of arrogant self-aggrandizement on the one hand, and self-beration on the other hand? Answer: Think your way through the philosophy of USA, especially in your intimate relationships. Be determined to always accept yourself as a "worthy" or "good" person *whether or not* you perform important tasks and relationships well—and *whether or not* significant other people accept you. Even more elegantly, use the unique REBT solution to the problem of self-evaluation by establishing important goals and purposes and only rating your thoughts, feelings, and actions in terms of these aims, and not globally rating yourself, your essence, your being, or your person at all. We shall keep returning to this point again. But let's stop here to complete more exercises and be more specific.

Exercise 3C: REBT's Famous Shame-Attacking Exercise

I (Dr. Ellis) vaguely realized when I practiced psychoanalysis in the late 1940s and early 1950s that feelings of shame, embarrassment, and humiliation were the essence of much—no, not all—human disturbance. When you are really ashamed of something you have "foolishly" done or of some "good" thing you have thought of doing but "cowardly" refrained from executing, you are almost always criticizing your "bad" behavior. You may well be right. To dress "ridiculously" when with your partner or to "stupidly" fail to give support when he or she is in trouble *will* often bring on censure, penalties, and disruption to the relationship. So, noting this, you'd better feel moderately abashed and push yourself to act differently next time. As a social creature and a would-be partner, use caution and vigilance.

Deep-seated shame or humiliation, however, usually adds some Irrational Beliefs (IBs) to create disturbances that we described above. First, especially when your partner criticizes your "ridiculous" dress or your lack of support, you feel ashamed of *it*—your "wrong" and "dislikable" *behavior*. Good. But, simultaneously, you put *yourself* down for your "foolish" or "bad" acts and feel ashamed of *yourself*. Quite a jump! Actually, your partner may only be criticizing what you've *done*. But you take it as criticism of *you* and agree that *you* are "bad" for doing *it*. A very neurotic overgeneralization. Deadly.

Second, you often horrify yourself about the *discomfort* of the "shameful" situation. You hate the *hassles* of defending your actions, of arguing with your mate, of being scorned, of correcting your behavior, and so forth. You define these hassles as *too* hard, tell yourself you *can't stand* them, insist that they are *awful*. So, in addition to making yourself feel ego-anxiety, you also create considerable discomfort-anxiety or low frustration tolerance (LFT).

Noting this, when I gave REBT group marathons in the 1960s, I invented some shame-attacking exercises that members of the group could risk doing, and dare being looked down upon for performing, during the marathon. For example, asking another member for a special personal encounter, removing some of one's clothing, or taking the risk of criticizing another's participation in the marathon.

My shame-attacking exercises during the REBT marathons worked so well that I added them to my regular weekly group therapy procedures, as well as to my individual therapy sessions. Usually, I give them as homework assignments and check later to see whether they are actually carried out, what results are experienced during and after doing them, and whether the participants became significantly less ashamed in their real lives. To date, many thousands of REBT-oriented people have done these shame-attacking exercises all over the world; and so many favorable results have been reported that they have been widely incorporated into cognitive behavior therapy (CBT) and into many other kinds of active-directive treatments of anxiety, shame, shyness, and other aspects of self-downing and low frustration tolerance.

Here are guidelines for your trying some shame-attacking exercises:

Pick some action that you would be ashamed to do, and especially to be observed doing by others. Make sure that you don't harm anyone else by doing this "shameful" act. Don't, for example, slap anybody in the face or really intrude on their privacy. Also, don't do anything that would harm yourself—such as walking naked in public or picking a fight with someone.

Give the matter of shame some deep thought and see that it usually consists of publicly doing something foolish or stupid, being viewed critically for doing it, and putting yourself, as a person, down for your poor behavior. So you have the *choice* of only rationally feeling ashamed—meaning, sorry or disappointed—about your "foolish" or "shameful" behavior *or* agreeing with your critics that you are less worthy as a person for behaving "shamefully." Decide that you will deliberately do the act you now think of as being "shameful" while *not* downing yourself, as a person, for doing it.

When you clearly see the difference between criticizing your "shameful" *act* and berating *yourself* for doing it, force yourself to do this act—preferably implosively, several times within a short period. If you complete the "embarrassing" act, see how you feel, and if you at first feel ashamed, work on your thoughts and feelings to minimize or eliminate the shame. If you fail to do it, work on not feeling ashamed of yourself for failing!

Before, during, and after your "shameful" act, you can think of rational coping self-statements and do your best to believe them. Such as:

"I can always fully accept *myself* even when I act foolishly and other people put me down."

"I don't like other people criticizing me and seeing me as a fool. But I never have to agree with them. I don't *need* their approval."

"My behavior is not bad in the sense of being immoral but even if it were, or were considered so, it makes me a *person who* is acting immorally and had better stop doing so. It doesn't make me a *wicked, evil person.*"

"I will most likely suffer very little reprisals for doing this "shameful" act and can gain greatly by giving myself unconditional self-acceptance (USA)."

Preferably, do a number of "shameful" acts until you consistently begin to feel—before, during, and after doing them—sorry, regretful, and disappointed about the censure you may get, but *not* ashamed, humiliated, embarrassed, or depressed. You can feel *good* about actually doing these exercises and conquering your own self-downing while doing them because you're doing them to *help* yourself. But, at worst, make yourself feel displeased with some of the criticism you get, but not disappointed or displeased with *you.*

Exercise 3D: Rational Emotive Imagery

Since its beginning in 1955, REBT has included a number of cognitive exercises in addition to its active-directive: Disputing (D) of people's Irrational Beliefs (IBs). One of these is imagery techniques, such as positive imagery or positive visualization.

In 1971, Maxie C. Maultsby, Jr., a creative psychiatrist who had studied REBT with me for a month in New York, in 1968, combined REBT's use of imagery with a highly emotive procedure and named the combination Rational Emotive Imagery (REI). I immediately saw that REI was a valuable addition to REBT, but because Maxie's original use of it overlapped too much with REBT Disputing of IBs, I kept the imagery and the emotive aspects of it and didn't focus as much as he did, at the same time, on showing my clients how to Dispute their Irrational Beliefs. I do this separately, usually before using REI.

I have used REI thousands of times with my clients and with my workshop participants. My version follows, and you may particularly find it useful to help you and your partner work to acquire un-conditional self-acceptance (USA). Here is a set of instructions that I frequently give to my clients at my famous Friday Night Work-shops and on other occasions.

Close your eyes and vividly imagine one of the worst things that you fear might happen to you—such as your partner telling you how impossible you are in several important respects, saying that no good mate will ever stay with you, and that you will soon wind up being totally alone forever. Vividly imagine that this grim event is actually happening and let yourself feel very negative about it. Feel whatever you feel—such as panicked, depressed, or enraged.

Can you vividly imagine that this very bad event is actually hap-pening? I'm sure that you can. All right, I see that you said, "Yes." Good! How do you actually feel *right now* as you vividly imagine this unfortunate event? How do you spontaneously feel?

(The person almost always replies, "Very anxious." Or, "Quite depressed." Or, "Extremely angry.")

Good. Get in touch with your feeling. Really feel it! Feel it as strongly as you can. Feel it, feel it, feel it! Are you now strongly feel-ing it?

(The person almost always responds, "Yes, I really do. I feel quite upset.")

Good. Now I want you to keep the same image—don't change it in any way. Keep the same image in your mind. But now work on your disturbed feeling and change it, as you are definitely able to do, to a healthy negative feeling—such as keen sorrow or regret. You can control your emotions, though often, not what happens to you. So make yourself, really make yourself, feel very sorry, very re-gretful about the bad things you are imagining happening to you. Only sorry and regretful about what's happening—not depressed, not self-hating. Only sorry and regretful—which you can definitely do.

(I usually wait a few minutes for the person to change her or his feeling from an unhealthy to a healthy negative emotion. You can wait for yourself to do this.)

Fine! Now what did you *do* to change your feeling? How did you change it?

(I deliberately do *not* ask the person, "What did you *tell yourself* to change your feeling?" For then they might not have really changed it but have figured out, from my leading question, that they're *supposed to* tell themselves something to change it. This makes it too easy for them to give the "right" answer, even if they don't really believe it. It also makes the REI technique too much like Disputing and answering with rational coping self-statements. It then may lose its emotive quality.)

I can tell by the person's answer whether he or she really has changed his or her unhealthy negative feeling to a healthy negative feeling. If they have, they give a rational coping self-statement that they have figured out for themselves, such as "I hate losing my *partner* but I do not hate *myself* for losing him or her." "Too bad that my partner is unfairly putting me down, but that's her or his way—which I don't agree with. He or she is a fallible human who is acting unfairly but is *not* a rotten person."

When you do REI and come up with a suitable rational coping self-statement that leads you to feel healthily rather than unhealthily negative, you repeat this at least once a day for thirty days, using the same or additional coping statements to change your disturbed feeling. If you do this properly and consistently, you soon train yourself to come up with automatic and spontaneous healthy negative feelings, instead of self-defeating ones, when you imagine very bad Activating Events or when they actually do occur.

You may have difficulty, at first, with this exercise. But if you keep doing it, you will start to see that your unhealthy negative feelings largely stem from your IBs—from the self-defeating statements that you tell yourself; and that you can always change them to healthy negative feelings by using rational coping self-statements. Then you don't *completely* control your self-sabotaging feelings, but you give yourself much more ability to call the shots on them!

4

Trying It Out Before Commitment

As we start this chapter, let's review what we have covered so far about ways to relate successfully to another individual. Although a relationship could be any kind of twosome, most people seek help on romance and erotic coupling. Why? Because our culture emphasizes romance and also because many assume (often falsely) that they can competently handle non-romantic relationships. If you are entering a business partnership, you take great care to inspect your potential partner's knowledge and skills in this field, but you may take for granted the problems that will arise from relating to him or her on a personal level. When things turn sour in this non-romantic situation, you'll probably turn to experts in your field to tell you what went wrong rather than examine how you and your partner related badly.

So while most of you may focus on romantic and erotic coupling, we shall still emphasize those problems that stem from matters other than sex and romance. Almost all of the ways we will suggest for improving close personal relationships can be applied to non-romantic and non-erotic couples, to the married and unmarried, and to straights and gays.

The toughest block to functioning effectively in couplehood is almost everyone's foolish tendency to rate self and others as total persons. REBT practitioners valiantly strive to help individuals and couples to focus on improving their *behaviors* rather than on rating their *selves* or other *people*. REBT teaches that long-term and not short-term satisfaction is the best guide to improvement; and it stresses the importance of beliefs in helping you change your ineffective functioning.

In chapter 3, with the help of Heather's and George's session, we saw how two people can begin to face, understand, and deal with some of the almost inevitable problems of couplehood, such as making themselves nondefensive, authentic, and unperfectionistic.

Now we will explore some ways that people who are tentatively living together can improve their relationship and test the possibility of a long-term commitment. In our earlier book, *A Guide to Successful Marriage*, commitment meant marriage. While it still means that to some people, our culture has changed so much in the last few decades that couples may or may not have marriage in mind even though they intend to live together permanently.

Couples who live together may do so for several reasons: (1) they are gay; (2) one or both is still legally married to someone else; (3) their relationship is nonsexual, so marriage seems inappropriate; (4) the advantages of marriage (greater community acceptance and legal and economic advantages, such as joint health insurance) are outweighed by the disadvantages (restrictions on individual freedom). This may especially be true when people decide to mate without having any children. Those who live together without intent to marry may be realistic, while some may mainly have irrational fears of being legally wed.

In addressing people today on "Living Together in Unfettered Love," we often bring out the following points. For one, "love conquers all." How many of you still believe that? Fewer, no doubt, than your parents' generation, but it is not a completely dopey idea when you take some of the absolutism away. How about, "love can help a hell of a lot?" Caring deeply for another person (which is how we're defining "love") can help you overcome some of the difficulties of mating. We say "difficulties" because most of us have never learned, even in our original families, how to relate warmly and understandingly to others. Many of us grow up in conditions where family members pretend to be warm and understanding and then pretend that they are not pretending. This *double pretend* may constitute deep-seated *denial*, because the pretender is often unaware of his or her real feelings.

How do you know if family members are unaware of their real feelings? And if you find double-pretending is indeed going on, how does that relate to our topic of living together in unfettered love? We tend to emerge from our original families with love quite fettered—in a kind of double bind of double pretend. So to unfetter ourselves, we had better first accept our possible fettering.

To reveal our pretenses abut loving those we blithely suppose that we do love, we need to be skeptical of our alleged feelings and probe to see how realistic they are. We can also look for the occasional flashes of awareness that break through our denial of our pretenses. In clinical work, the evidence for pretend and double pretend, especially in matters of love, is often vague. But we can often accept pretense as a helpful working hypothesis and try to change it to nonpretense whenever we discover it.

The question is, how do people emerge from a double-bind pretend and start living in loving couplehood with other persons who may be similarly unaware of their pretending? The answer is that usually they don't. But because they have learned to pretend so well, they may stay together for quite a long time. Most of them used to get married and transmit the same patterns of pretense to their offspring, generation after generation. At least some of you in this generation are testing out living together before launching such major legal and social commitments as marriage and parenthood.

Do we approve of a couple living together before marriage? Definitely yes, but not just "before marriage." In the last two or three decades a lot of people (excluding religious and political extremists, but including some conservatives) have changed their attitudes toward unmarried couples who live together. They have gone from thinking "Let's jail them as moral criminals" to at least "Let's not talk about it or interfere." Personally, we approve of two persons living together in a close relationship even if marriage is never to be considered. That means a woman and a man, a woman and a woman, or a man and a man, as long as the two are consenting adults—consenting to living together; not necessarily consenting to sex as sexual interest and/or activity may or may not be present.

That doesn't mean that we are necessarily against two people under eighteen living together (providing it can be responsibly worked out within legal and social frameworks, as it sometimes can). Nor that we are against more than two people taking a whack at living together except that threesomes and foursomes are so much more complicated than twosomes that we highly recommend trying with two first.

Sex generally plays a role in human interaction when love is involved, and although sex and love are not interchangeable, the two can affect each other when it comes to relationships. We use the term "love" to refer to intense caring for another human. Sex (erotic desire and activity) may often interfere with or distract from deep love. How? Sometimes if you really concentrate on how much you deeply *care* for your sexual partner, you may well interfere with—not enhance—your and his or her erotic satisfaction. If so, you may focus too much on your partner's satisfaction and not enough on your own; or you may be so tender and "nice" that you may neglect powerful sex urges that would help stimulate your partner.

When we work with a couple trying to achieve a close personal relationship, each member of which has emerged from the frequent family background of phony caring, we often say, "You don't *have* to love each other, but it would probably help a hell of a lot if you learned to do so." And they say: "Yeah, sounds lovely. How do we do it?" What do we then reply?

We show people how to behave more lovingly with each other and how not to rate each other as total persons. We try to help each of them see how they can be more affectionate toward their partner and how not to focus on the "goodness" or "badness" of the other person. That is the essence of the REBT view of unconditionally accepting and therefore being able to better love each other.

We encourage people to *behave* more lovingly toward their partner rather than asking, "How can I be a great lover?" or "Why do I have such an asshole of a partner who fails to meet my every wish?" or "If my stupid parents had been more genuinely affectionate wouldn't I now be a truly loving person?" If people can concentrate on seeing how they can improve their loving behavior, they will often make real progress.

In the all-too-usual family, the child lives with angry, depressed, or indifferent parents who *say* they are interested and loving. They instruct the child, "Be a nicer boy or girl. Only a bad child would eat up all the cookies. So you know what *you* are!" Many children learn to pretend that they do not have horrendous inner urges, such as the urge to gobble up all the goodies in sight. But in order to convince themselves they are not "bad children" they double-pretend—that is, pretend that they are not pretending. Otherwise, they may see themselves as "bad persons" for the rest of their lives.

When we say to an individual in couple therapy, "Try to behave more lovingly toward your partner," we are not duplicating the pathology of this kind of family scene. This is why. First, each partner is asked to describe his or her thoughts, feelings, perceptions, and actions in a problematic couple situation. Next, both may be asked to close their eyes and focus on that "awful" situation and to silently let their reactions have full sway. After, they are encouraged, while their eyes are still closed, to see if each can imagine ways of behaving more lovingly toward the other in a similar future situation. Finally, both are asked to describe how they modified their imagined behavior change with as little reference as possible to how they think the other person might react to this change.

Is this imagined change still somewhat phony and superficial? Possibly, but it is still very different from what most people experienced in developing undesirable and unloving behaviors in earlier interactions. Part of its lingering artificiality is that both partners may make some imaginative changes to impress the other one. But using REBT for couples helps many couples to wipe out other stimuli and to focus intensively on ways of improving their own behavior. The effect of each partner's saying in front of the other how he or she would behave more lovingly is often very positively reinforcing. They remember what they said; they remember that they thought it up themselves with no pressure from anyone else; and they are likely to try to do their damnedest to actually function that way.

REBT, however, goes even further. It also points out the harmful nature of perfectionism. It describes how couples have great difficulty in changing their habits. It helps people to give up their unrealistic expectations and to cherish even their small successes at becoming more loving.

Can these procedures that work with couples also be used to make behavioral changes not related to lovingness? Yes, they often can be. As REBT has noted since the 1950s, people not only learn to be unloving in their original families, but just about all people have strong innate or biological tendencies to disturb themselves, and thereby to disrupt their relationships.

What people need to look at and do something about is how well or badly their behavior fulfills the purpose of the relationship they want. What is that purpose? Just to have fun? It's presumably more than that or they typically would not consider living together.

Falling in love with someone causes readjustments in your life, and therefore, you and your mate should think long and hard about what you are trying to accomplish in this living-together situation. This arrangement is *not* unfettered love! So look at your behavior to see how it fits in with your purposes. Then work at improving your communication and problem-solving skills.

Sound difficult? Not exactly, but an REBT way of life *does* take extra effort. It's well worth it, though, when it increases satisfaction in living. It usually brings more love and more fun for individuals and couples alike. Totally unfettered? Hell, no—because it takes planning and problem-solving. This shatters the myth that fun should be something that just happens and that somehow the greatest joy is to have no responsibility laid on you to do anything at all. Even when you have interesting and enjoyable experiences as a result of your special efforts, you may still believe that "the ideal" is do-nothingness. One of the benefits that you can get from a close personal relationship is that both you and your partner reinforce each other in living a more rational, realistic, and satisfying life.

EXERCISES

Up to now, we have mainly been emphasizing how to be honest with yourself and your partner—that is, how to stop pretending that you *really* care and that you are *not* pretending. Great stuff! But your honesty is often blocked by your direly *needing*, instead of healthily *wanting*, your partner's (and other people's) approval and by your attaching your worth as a person to how much acceptance you get.

Pretending that you're not pretending goes, again, with defensiveness, inauthenticity, and perfectionism. Antidote? Unconditional self-acceptance, which can be marvelous *if* you work to achieve it.

Seeing through your own and your partner's possible dishonesty often requires doing things the hard way—living together to see how both of you actually react to the difficulties of everyday life as a couple.

Let's take it a step further. Suppose that you do live together or otherwise get to really know each other and that you do find, first, that you both are talented pretenders and, second, that you react badly to the rigors of Holy Couplehood. Quite annoying. Almost enraging. Now, what do you do about *that?*

Answer: Discover and dispute the second main set of IBs that lead to fury about your partner's dishonesty and difficulties and to experience low frustration tolerance (LFT), awfulizing, and I-can't-stand-it-itis about the "horrible" hassles of intimate living. So far, we have mainly given you exercises to combat your feelings of wormhood. Now it's time for exercises that uproot your rage and then, later on, ones to reduce your LFT.

Exercise 4A: Acknowledging Your Highly Conditional Acceptance of Your Partner

Naturally you love your partner, enjoy being with him or her, and do many caring things to show your love. But is that *all?* If you are human, you also at times hate your mate, feel disgust for her or him, would even like to kill that person. How can you honestly admit this? Examine Sample Practice Sheet 4A, give it some deep thought, then forcibly and probably painfully tackle Actual Practice Sheet 4A. Be honest about what you see!

Sample Exercise 4A: Acknowledging Your Highly Conditional Acceptance of Your Partner

Partner's Failings and Mistreatment of Me	My Disturbed Feelings and Actions About My Partner's Failings and Mistreatment of Me
Partner is very untidy.	Pissed off. Keep nagging him or her to be tidier.
Partner severely criticizes me.	Self-pity and self-downing. Defensiveness. Look for things to lambaste him or her about.
Partner is careless about money and spends too much.	Feel aghast when bills come in. Lecture partner steadily about this. Think he or she is a damned baby.
Partner is often late to appointments and makes me late.	Keep yelling at him or her. Angrily leave without her or him. Keep seething about this and spoil our outings.
Partner gives me much less sex than I want.	Angrily refuse to have any sex. Tell partner she or he is a basket case for being sexless. Feel very hurt.
Partner lies to me about important things.	Fume and froth and accuse him or her of always lying. Refuse to discuss reasons for lying, and feel there is *no* excuse except death.

Exercise 4A

My Partner's Failings and Mistreatment of Me	My Disturbed Feelings and Actions About My Partner's Failings and Mistreatment of Me
_____	_____
_____	_____
_____	_____
_____	_____
_____	_____
_____	_____
_____	_____
_____	_____
_____	_____
_____	_____
_____	_____
_____	_____
_____	_____
_____	_____
_____	_____
_____	_____

*Sample Exercise 4B: Irrational Beliefs (IBs) That Encourage My
Disturbed Feelings and Actions About My Partner's Failings and
Mistreatment of Me*

My Disturbed Feelings and Actions About My Partner's Failings and Mistreatment of Me	My Irrational Beliefs (IBs), Which Encourage My Disturbed Feelings and Actions About My Partner's Failings and Mistreatment of Me
Pissed off about his or her untidiness. Keep nagging him or her all the time. Self-pity and self-downing when partner criticizes me.	He or she *must not* be untidy! That seriously handicaps me and is unfair. She or he *must* be fair! Woe is me! After all I do for him or her! I must be an incompetent person if this criticism is correct. If my partner really loved me, he or she could never be so critical.
Feel aghast when my partner spends more than we have. Lecture him or her for being a damned baby.	S/he is dishonest and totally rotten for treating me this way! How incredibly idiotic! S/he is a baby who never faces reality! After I go out of my way to save, my partner should not get us into debt!
Keep yelling at partner for always being late to appointments. Keep seething and spoil our outings.	How can he or she be that rotten way! It's so easy to plan to be on time and there's no excuse for him or her not to be! S/he is a thoroughly disorganized and rotten person!
Angrily refuse to have any sex and tell partner s/he is a basket case when my partner gives me less sex than I want.	I'll fix his or her wagon! S/he could easily have more sex with me and is an inconsiderate, unloving, lousy person for refusing to have it!

Exercise 4B (cont.)

My Disturbed Feelings and Actions About My Partner's Failings and Mistreatment of Me	My Irrational Beliefs (IBs), Which Encourage My Disturbed Feelings and Actions About My Partner's Failings and Mistreatment of Me
Fume and froth when partner lies to me about important things. Feel there is no excuse for this.	What a complete liar s/he is! A hopeless liar who can't ever tell the truth completely does me in—as a loving partner never should!

Exercise 4B

My Disturbed Feelings and Actions About My Partner's Failings and Mistreatment of Me	My Irrational Beliefs (IBs) That Encourage My Disturbed Feelings and Actions About My Partner's Failings and Mistreatment of Me
_____	_____
_____	_____
_____	_____
_____	_____
_____	_____
_____	_____
_____	_____
_____	_____
_____	_____
_____	_____
_____	_____
_____	_____
_____	_____
_____	_____

Sample Exercise 4C: Rational Coping Self-Statements to Minimize My Irrational Beliefs (IBs) About My Partner's Failings and Mistreatment of Me

My Irrational Beliefs (IBs) About My Partner's Failings and Mistreatment of Me	Rational Coping Self-Statements I Can Use to Minimize My Irrational Beliefs (IBs)
My partner *must not* be untidy! That seriously handicaps me and is unfair. S/he *must* be fair and be tidy!	My partner is a fallible human who has every right to be untidy. Yes, his/her untidiness may seriously handicap me and may be unfair. But unfairness must exist when it exists and untidiness is quite disadvantageous but not *horrible*. Let me see if I can *un*-angrily help him/her to change.
Woe is me! After all I do for my partner s/he must not severely criticize me. I must be an incompetent person if this criticism is correct. If s/he really loved me this would never happen. S/he is dishonest and totally rotten for treating me this way!	No matter how well I treat my partner s/he can still easily criticize me. That may be his/her nature! This criticism never makes me an incompetent person—even if it is correct. Just a person who at times *acts* incompetently. Even if my partner really loves me, s/he can still be over-critical and usually honest about my failings. This may be rotten, but s/he is not a *rotten person*.
How incredibly idiotic it is when my partner overspends! S/he is a baby who never faces reality! After I go out of my way to save, s/he must never get us into debt!	Foolish overspending is hardly incredible but actually fairly common. My partner is acting childish in that respect but is not a total baby who never faces reality. S/he is only *sometimes* unrealistic. It's good that I go out of my way to save, but that doesn't *make* her/him a sensible spender who never gets us into debt. Too bad!—but s/he has several other good traits.

Exercise 4C (cont.)

My Irrational Beliefs (IBs) About My Partner's Failings and Mistreatment of Me	Rational Coping Self-Statements I Can Use to Minimize My Irrational Beliefs (IBs)
How can s/he be this rotten way—always being late to appointments? Because it's so easy to plan to be on time, s/he has no excuse for not arranging to be! My partner is a thoroughly disorganized and rotten person!	My partner has no trouble—alas!—in acting this rotten way. That's the way s/he often is. Even though I find it easy to plan to be on time my partner seems to find it very hard to arrange this. S/he is disorganized in this respect but does many other things well and is obviously not a disorganized rotten *person.*
I'll fix my partner's wagon when s/he gives me less sex than I want. S/he could easily have more sex with me and is an inconsiderate, unloving, lousy person for refusing to have sex!	It's really silly if I try to hostilely fix my partner's wagon—because then I'll get less sex! S/he can't *easily* have more sex with me—otherwise s/he would probably have it. S/he may still be considerate and loving, but have several good reasons for refusing to have more sex. Perhaps he/she is acting rottenly *in this* respect, but is surely not a rotten lousy person.
My partner is a complete liar when s/he lies to me about important things—a hopeless liar who *can't* ever tell the truth! S/he completely does me in—as a loving partner never should!	My partner lies about some important things but is obviously not a *complete* liar who lies about *everything.* S/he most probably is *not* a hopeless liar and *can* tell the truth—but for certain reasons, chooses to do otherwise at times. S/he handicaps me somewhat by lying but hardly *completely* does me in. S/he *should* lie right now, because that is his/her present way. Loving partners *still* sometimes lie—and they, too, must right now be the way that they are. Too bad!

Exercise 4C

My Irrational Beliefs (IBs) About My Partner's Failings and Mistreatment of Me	Rational Coping Self-Statements I Can Use to Minimize My Irrational Beliefs (IBs)

5

Communicating and Problem-Solving as a Couple

So far, we haven't shown how you and your partner can teach yourselves to focus on your own loving behavior. As with many REBT procedures, you can do this most effectively outside of therapy, during homework time. In this chapter we'll try to give clear examples of how couples can improve their communication and problem-solving skills in and out of the therapy situation.

We have found that no matter how experienced couples may be in the art of communicating, they should assume that they often do not successfully transmit the messages they think they are transmitting to each other. If you do already make such assumptions, some of the communication exercises we recommend may at first seem a bit kindergartenish. So it was with Jan and Ed, who I (Dr. Harper) saw for couples therapy, and who I tried to get to listen to each other:

Ed: You mean I am supposed to repeat after Jan what she has just said? And then she's supposed to say to me: "Hey, Ed, do I hear you correctly as saying you'd like me to pass the butter?"

R.A.H.: If butter-passing was an area in which the two of you had difficulty understanding each other, we might well begin there. As I understand the two of you, your problems are somewhat different, so I'd like to start with this exercise to learn a little bit more about your situation. Let's ask Jan to start with something that is really troubling her, and then the two of you can replay the other's requests back and forth.

Jan: Well, the thing that troubles me the most is: Ed, I don't think you really take me seriously as an equal.

Ed: Oh, crap! Okay, I'll play the game. Jan, I hear you saying that you don't think I really take you seriously as an equal.

Jan: Yeah, that's what I said. But I hear you interpreting that what's troubling me is a lot of crap and that this is all an idiotic game.

Ed: You heard me all right, sweet buns.

Jan: Defense rests! (She turns to me.) He apparently doesn't understand that he just proved that what troubles me is true. (I interrupt to tell Jan to talk to Ed.) Okay, can't you see that by calling my troubles "crap," and by not taking seriously what the therapist prescribed as an exercise to help us understand better what the other person is trying to communicate, *and* by calling me sweet buns, you are proving to me the very thing that troubles me most, namely— you dumb bastard that I unfortunately love—that you don't relate to me as an equal?

R.A.H.: Before we get to Ed's response, let's examine why it might well be negative. Although Jan's summary analysis was splendid, she first labeled Ed as a dumb bastard (even if she was kidding), and then asserted that she *unfortunately* loved him. She thereby made it almost certain for Ed to be distracted from her main message. Jan, please deliver your main message again in as close as you can to the same words as you used before. (Jan does so.)

Ed: I heard your main message all right. You are seriously troubled that I don't treat you as an equal. I don't think you are right, but I want to work it out with you so you feel that I do treat you as an equal.

R.A.H.: Splendid! Ed, you have correctly discerned that you do not have to agree with Jan in order to come to clearly understand what is troubling her. But you have also come up with a very positive attitude of wanting to work with Jan so that she doesn't feel seriously troubled. An important principle can be generalized here:

Whenever one person in an intimate relationship experiences a problem, then (regardless of the differing view of the partner) *a problem does indeed exist and problem-solving is highly desirable.* It is easy for any of us in a couple relationship to decide, "I'm right, and he or she is crazy." This makes problem-solving *more* difficult!

But let's not lose sight right now of this simple exercise. Your first step is to satisfy each other *that you understand your partner's problems.* I'd like both of you to try, as your first homework assignment, to identify three problems, and by going through this first step with each of them, to make sure that you both understand the other's problem. Then at the next session, you will report back what happened. In fairness, I'd suggest that one extra problem be contributed by Ed, because Jan has already raised one.

In the time that remains for this session, let's take Jan's problem and see if we can get beyond the first step. I am going to have both of you try two brief exercises that we frequently use in REBT couples therapy. Please close your eyes. Now, Jan, will you imagine what *you* (not Ed, but *you*) could do to change any of your thoughts, perceptions, feelings, or actions to make your relationship a more equal one? In the meantime, Ed, focus on how you could alter *any* of your thoughts, perceptions, feelings, or actions to help Jan experience more equality in relating to you? Each of you is to focus on your *own* behavior (keeping your eyes closed).

(Three minutes later.) Okay, let's hear from Jan first. Both of you please keep your eyes closed until each of you has reported what you have thought and felt in the last three minutes. Now we'll move to exercise two. Be sure you still fully report to each other what you have thought and felt as you did in the previous exercise.

Jan: Yeah, well, I sort of see why Ed says these exercises are childish, but they really get to me. I focused on my behavior the way you told us to do and realized and felt that what I had really been saying by my reactions to Ed is that I feel insecure in this relationship. So the way I can help equalize things is to feel less insecure, and the way I can do that is to stop insisting that I absolutely must control how things go. Either we go for the long haul, or we don't. Either he thinks I'm an equal, or he doesn't. And, if in my non-insecure (if that's a word) judgment, he doesn't—then screw him, the haul is over, and I move on to another relationship. Ed was right in a sense to say my equality pitch was crap because I keep thinking he *has* to treat me equally and *has* to feel a certain way about me, and that the relationship *has* to work out or my world will come to an end. Now, after my three minutes of looking at my reactions, I, too, would say crap to all that. So I'm going to work on my demands and the insecurity I create with them and I'm going to try to point my behavior toward enjoying this relationship.

Ed: Wow! I take back whatever I said about these being idiotic exercises. I had a hard time not opening my eyes to make sure that was still Jan using Jan's voice. It's hard for me now to stick to my own report and not respond to what Jan said, which I think was terrific. But my focus was along the line that I've been something of a defensive asshole and I have not been willing to consider any-thing—including what I now consider these simple *and* valuable ex-ercises—that did not fit within my rigid scheme. My contribution to helping Jan think and feel that I treat her as an equal will be to refuse to dismiss anything she says as crap. First, I'll listen to her and ask for confirmation: "Is this what I hear you saying?" Then I'm going to say: "Hey, please excuse me a few minutes, Jan, while I take a swig or two of exercise one." And then I will focus conscientiously on my own behavior when Jan has a problem with me, just as I have tried to do this time. Then I'll go on to exercise two and tell Jan ex-actly what I thought and felt that *I* could do when I did exercise one to change my feelings and behaviors that she wanted me to change.

R.A.H.: Good! You have both just indicated how you can do these two exercises as homework assignments. You have also indi-cated how you can have some fun with these exercises by not just seeing them as grim assignments, but as a way of communicating better, as a means to problem-solving and real enjoyment.

Let me make sure, though, that you both understand that you are free to react to what the other one reports in exercise two. But it is preferable, as both of you realized, to wait until the other's report has been made. Then there is less chance of your own focusing on self-change getting blurred by your emotional reactions to the other's report. The purpose of both exercises is to improve your communication and assist your problem-solving. Your reactions to each other's contributions are quite desirable.

Since our time is up for today, most of your reactions to what the other one has said will have to be done at home or discussed here next week. Let me caution that human endeavors—including these exercises—tend to be imperfect, so your first exercise may leave you still unsure that your partner understands your problems. The second exercise may often fail to quickly create the new behaviors that lead to the problem-solving you arrived at today.

Some problems are very hard to crack, so if you expect that success will always be quick and easy, you may give up. Finding solutions often takes long hard work, but with persistence, most problems *can* be solved. Occasionally, however, you may end up with the undesirable "resolution" of "good-bye relationship." But even that, though hardly preferable, need not be viewed as "horrible" and "awful." Because today you both seem well on your way to problem-solving. And if you are both willing to work at this, you can most likely achieve an enjoyable close relationship—and yes, even if you always have some important differences.

I tried to caution Jan and Ed against overconfidence, which can easily arise from early success and lead to giving up when real tough problems arise. Conversely, couples often get discouraged when their first efforts to handle a difficulty fall flat. Sometimes one or both parties deny the existence of a problem (you remember George in chapter two). Others pessimistically and rigidly hold that nothing can be done to improve their situation.

These attitudinal and emotional problems need to be remedied before incompatibilities can be resolved. Even with problem deniers and neurotic pessimists, persistent use of both exercises performed with Jan and Ed can bring good results.

In that case, Jan and Ed's agreeing that they could solve their problems and that each of them could alter his/her thoughts, feelings, perceptions, and actions was a tremendous help. Although it may not seem the case to some readers, it is still a radical concept—

even in psychotherapy circles—that people are able to regulate their own lives instead of letting themselves be driven by organic, unconscious, social, or cosmic forces. "You must take me as I am" and "That's just the way I am" (and, hence, unchangeable) are strongly held beliefs of many partners. The two exercises just demonstrated showed that good results can occur when neither individual holds strongly to the common belief that misery is forced on him/her by outside people or events. These same two exercises can powerfully help partners overcome their underlying IBs about themselves and each other.

Making sure that both understand each other's perceptions of problems and focusing on changing each of their own problem behaviors, and not merely their partner's problem behaviors, are helpful in solving mating difficulties. But, by doing this, couples hardly always and automatically end up with a heavenly relationship. Just as we observed that love does not necessarily conquer all in chapter three, so can we admit the same for these two REBT communication and problem-solving exercises. What else can be done to improve unheavenly relationships? Let's return to Ed and Jan in the middle of their second session.

Jan: I hate to bring this up—especially since we are solving our equal treatment problem and because we are both enthusiastic about how well the two exercises you taught us are working—but is this it? Is this all we have to do?

R.A.H.: If you hadn't brought this up yourself, I would have mentioned it soon. No, this is not a perfect ending, either for your relationship or for therapy. What we've done up to now is to get the train (that is, the relationship) on the track and work out ways to keep it on track. Your love for each other—and by that I mean your deep caring for each other and not the erotic charges you give each other—will contribute greatly to your staying on track, too. When I sort of reprimanded Jan in our last session for saying that she loved you, Ed, it was because we were trying to concentrate on a different kind of communication. Love is not only an important thing to communicate to each other, but it can also help keep you interested in and contribute solutions to your problems. There's scarcely anything better for any relationship than plenty of deep caring.

Ed: When Jan asked if this is it, I think she was reflecting that we were doing the two exercises and becoming pretty damned good at problem-solving. But we were wondering whether a long-term application of this stuff would become boring as hell.

R.A.H.: For many people it well might! Those two exercises, now that you have had a week to use them as problem-solving procedures, can be put in the cupboard until the next serious communication difficulty occurs. It would help if you practiced the techniques a little just to make sure you keep them ready for possible troubles. But even working to resolve trouble can be tempered with humor and having fun—which are very good lubricants for problem-solving.

The third exercise is broader and deeper, and is to be pursued as a kind of perpetual homework assignment—practically never to be put in the cupboard. This consists of each of you asking yourself and discussing with each other, *"How can we make life more interesting and enjoyable?"*

Jan: Sounds great but also can be overdone.—"How can we get a bigger bang out of life and to hell with other people?"

R.A.H.: That's a short-term interpretation. Only if you take the lure of an easy and quick fix—of immediate gratification. Focusing on fixing yourselves quickly often does disregard the rights and pleasure of others. But realize that for you to find ways of making life more interesting and enjoyable takes thinking, problem-solving, discussing, planning, experimenting, rethinking, rediscussing, replanning, and re-experimenting. This is longer-term, and it is hard work, not a quick fix. Working at making your lives more interesting and enjoyable is an exercise that gets built into your very philosophy of life. The process itself often gets to be interesting and enjoyable and even downright exciting. But it calls for patience and persistence in trying to understand and deal with old habits of thinking, feeling, perceiving, and acting and to convert them into more effective habits. This third exercise is endless—it is a way of life—*and*, again, it is hard work. *But* you will often find that it brings more satisfaction than any other way of life I have ever heard about.

Ed: I can tell you that Jan and I will be living exercise three and not just preaching it. I think Jan's and my working so hard for a week on the first two exercises makes it easier for us to see that focusing on how we can make life more interesting and enjoyable won't be *too* hard for us. But I still agree with Jan that it sounds rather selfish.

R.A.H.: All I can do is assure you that it usually doesn't work out that way. First of all, I have found through the years that many of us are inclined to label other people as "selfish" whenever they don't do what we want them to do. We call people "selfish" when we think they *should* be behaving differently from the way they are behaving. Second, if you decide to do things the REBT way (that is, based on long-range interest rather than immediate gratification), you realistically consider the points of view of other people. You don't let others' feelings dominate you, but you consider how they will probably react to your decisions in both the short and long run. If you use longer-term self-interest as your guide you are less likely to smoke regularly or to practice your drums at 2:00 A.M. You will probably intrude less on other people's lives than some righteous reformer who is "unselfishly" trying to keep other people from having abortions or from viewing pornography.

Ed: Does that mean you are against reform?

R.A.H.: No, certainly not! The three of us are working right now to "reform" your lives and the ways you relate to one another. But you are here by consent and not by demand and control. We are trying to help you make changes that the three of us agree are desirable. The same cooperative process can be used in the broader community. If you want to use educational methods to try to *persuade* others not to view pornography or not to have abortions, that's quite different from violently trying to *prevent* them from doing so. But back to the two of you. Why would it be preferable to help you with your emotional problems while also working on your REBT exercises?

Jan: I suspect because our doubts, fears, and skepticism should be dealt with before we can really throw ourselves wholeheartedly into living the REBT way.

Ed: Yeah, I might even add that we've not only been removing some obstacles, as Jan points out, but we have begun experiencing the increased interest and enjoyment that comes from experimenting with this approach.

R.A.H.: Fine. What, again, would be a good homework assignment for next week?

Ed: And for the next zillion weeks, if I get the aim of exercise three straight: namely, look individually and as a couple for ways of improving the interest and enjoyment of our lives.

Jan: Right. And don't forget, Ed, we can concentrate on what's interesting and enjoyable on a long-term basis—and try to have barrels of fun while we are doing all this stuff! We can use exercises one and two in case we hit any problems. But we can have lots of laughs even with problems. Right?

R.A.H.: Very right! I highly endorse your fun-seeking slant. Jan gave a particularly neat and accurate summary of where we are and where we are trying to go. I think that both of you have not only been listening, but you have also been trying to apply what you're learning. However, you don't have to be just wide-eyed Ms. Gullible and Mr. Goody-Two-Shoes. As I've said before, this is tough stuff and not all sweetness and light. You'd better work at it!

Ed: I agree. I was thinking, even before Jan spoke: "Hey, what in hell have I gotten myself into with all this REBT stuff? Life used to be a breeze." But it wasn't, really, or we wouldn't be here. As I think I said a while ago—or maybe I just thought it, I'm not sure—I'm beginning to get a bang out of this whole approach and am willing to keep working at all three exercises, especially number three.

Jan: Me, too. I may not be an easy lay, as you once said, Ed, but I seem to be a sucker for REBT.

R.A.H.: You both sound committed to giving it your best shot. Try to avoid both perfectionism and easy discouragement, but practice exercises one and two if you slack off. In the meantime, happy exercise three! See you next week.

To show you how exercises one, two, and three can be effectively used in other kinds of relationship therapy, let me (Dr. Ellis) describe the case of José and Marella, who were at continued loggerheads as to how strict they should be with their eight-year-old son, Juan. José, reared in a conventional Mexican family, thought that they should be very strict, especially when Juan neglected his chores and avoided doing his homework. Marella was much more lenient and forgiving.

During this couple's first session with me, I explained some of the principles of REBT and showed them that Marella was angry at José for being *too* strict with Juan—which he absolutely *must not* be—and that José was furious at Marella for letting Juan "get away with murder" and not be as disciplined about his chores and his homework as he *absolutely should* be. She, thought José, was turning him into a "thug"—as she definitely *must not*. They agreed with me that they were *demanding*, not merely *wishing*, that the other "correctly" raise Juan. José was also insisting that their son be "a real, disciplined male," and was often enraged at him for not achieving this "necessary" goal. They agreed that they were both *mus*turbating, but I could see that they were giving only lip service to stopping it.

I started them on exercise one, listening to each other. I asked José to present his view of raising Juan to Marella. He said, "I want Juan to grow up to be a real *man*, not an undisciplined sissy like you want him to be. I'm angry that you're indulging him and turning him into a spoiled brat!"

Marella—naturally—bristled at this and immediately started to argue that José was trying to turn Juan into a male chauvinist pig—just like himself! I stopped her and insisted that she *just* repeat what she heard José say. After a few incorrect tries, she managed to say, "I hear you saying that you want Juan to grow up to be a real man and not a sissy like I want him to be. You're angry at me for spoiling him and supposedly turning Juan into a spoiled brat."

Pretty close to José's statement of his feelings, we agreed. "Now state how you feel," I told Marella, "and José, you carefully listen and repeat her view." Marella began, "José, you're much too strict with Juan. After all, he's only eight and will grow up to hate himself if you keep after him like you do. Maybe you want him to be a manly boy. But, hell, he's only a child! Call off your dogs!"

José listened carefully and repeated Marella's statement almost word for word. Then he added, "But he'd better be a little boy, not a wimp, right now!"

"None of that extra stuff!" I warned José. "Just repeat what you heard Marella say *without* saying anything extra, at least right now." He did so. I then gave Marella and José the homework assignment of each of them stating to the other partner three different problems that they had in their relationship, with the other repeating what they said until they both agreed that they really heard what their partner felt about their problems.

Then I gave José and Marella exercise two: "Close your eyes. Now will you, Marella, imagine what you (not José, but *you*) could do to curb your anger at José even though he continues to be very strict with Juan? How could *you* accept José with his present attitude, which you think is so wrong, and what could you tell yourself to reduce your anger at him? While you are doing this, will you, José, focus not on Marcella's thoughts, feelings, and actions about Juan and you, but only upon what you could tell yourself to do to accept her with her present attitude, which you think is so wrong? What could *you* do to reduce your anger at her? Both of you for the next few minutes are to work at changing your *own* attitudes and feelings about the other's so-called poor behavior. Keep your eyes closed now and use the next three minutes to focus on how you could change *yourself* about this problem you both have with each other."

After I gave them three minutes Marella reported: "That was hard! It took me almost a minute to focus on me, because I kept thinking of José and how *he* should change. But I kept at it, and finally thought that, first, I could make a real effort to see that he had a genuine point of view, genuine for him, even if I strongly disagreed with it. Second, I realized—as you showed us during our first session—that when I was angry at José I had a strong *must* that was helping make me angry. Not he, but my must, was the issue. So

I found it: "José *absolutely must not* oppose me about Juan, when I'm so right and he's so wrong!" I then began to see that it was highly *preferable* that José not oppose me about Juan, but there was *no* reason that he *had* to act preferably. As soon as I told myself that, much of my anger flew out the window. I even saw that José's intentions were good, though I did not agree with them."

José listened to Marella with amazement, then reported on his own three minutes: "Like Marella, I at first had trouble focusing on *me* because I was still enraged at *her* and even thought that she was deliberately handling Juan gently in order to upset me. But I saw that my focus was still on her and remembered your instructions, so I forced it back to me. I realized that by being angry, I was hurting myself, ruining my relationship with Marella, and maybe even being unfair to Juan—who is really a great kid and I love him a lot. I saw how anger was greatly raising my blood pressure, which is much too high already. So I quickly said to myself, 'This is stupid! I'd better stop it! Even if I'm right about being strict with Juan, I don't have to be *angrily* strict.' So I made myself relax by using breathing techniques, and resolved that hereafter I would spend a hell of a lot more time *un*making rather than *making* myself angry. That resolve immediately calmed me down—and then I began to think that maybe Marella had some good points after all. But I thought of her only after, as you told us to do, I first thought of how to change *me*."

José and Marella were both delighted with each other's carrying out of exercise two, and fully agreed that, as homework, they would try to do it with three more relationship problems. They did so and had an unusually good week in working on their anger about several other household, spending, and in-law problems. They weren't exactly cured, but achieved the insight that their anger largely stemmed from themselves, not their mate's "wrongness," and therefore they could almost always reduce it by taking a few minutes to see what each of them could do, with or without the other's help, to tackle it.

By sharing what each of them did in their work on themselves in exercise two, José and Marella got additional ideas on how to curb their own anger (as well as depression) and added to their repertoire of REBT useful techniques. Then I helped them proceed to exercise three: Asking themselves and discussing with each other "How can we make life more interesting and more enjoyable?"

Although they came to therapy at first only to overcome their anger and bickering about how to deal with Juan, they found that after this largely was alleviated, they automatically enjoyed many former pursuits—such as watching television—more. But energized by me to explore greater interests and enjoyments, they did some exploration and experimenting, and added to their active participations ballroom dancing, opera-going, and joining a regular discussion group. When I last heard from them, they were considering bird-watching!

No relationship, we repeat, is perfect. Until their son, Juan, became a teenager and was on his own, Marella and José still differed about how strictly to raise him. Differed, but didn't fight about it. Each of them partly willingly accepted, without liking, the other's child-raising notions and therefore made some suitable compromises.

EXERCISES FOR CHAPTER 5

This chapter showed how REBT is often specifically designed for couples (and family) therapy. In this chapter, Jan and Ed had a communication problem—*between* them. So both *together* were shown how to do two exercises to help resolve their problem.

Oddly enough, however, the first exercise they were taught focused on how each of them could work to change *himself* and *herself* along with their working together. This is what effective couple therapy almost always seems to do. The partners, naturally, talk to each other and, with the therapist's help, work on improving their *relationship*. Isn't that what they come for? Indeed!

However, unless at least one of the two—and preferably both—see themselves as somewhat mistaken and somewhat disturbed, little progress is likely to be made. They usually have *both* individual and coupled problems—not either/or. So REBT first tends to help each of them acknowledge, understand, and work at changing his or her problems—especially disturbances—which they may well *bring to* the relationship.

As I (Dr. Ellis) tell the professionals who attend my workshops on marital and family therapy, I assume that people like Jan and Ed have their own neurotic reactions and had them long before they met each other. These reactions do not necessarily make them incompatible—but they certainly help to do so!

REBT couple counseling, therefore, usually first highlights some of each individual's personal difficulties—as Dr. Harper gently did with Ed and Jan. Before he tried to help one communicate with the other (as he did in the second REBT exercise he gave them), he instructed them to get into their own heads and communicate carefully with themselves. They did this by first acknowledging that they *could* act better with each other and second, by imagining some methods of actually doing so.

Note the inevitable interaction here between Ed and Jan's self-focus and other-focus. Their goal was to figure out how to improve their *relationship*. So, almost perversely, they first got into their *own* thoughts and feelings. But—ah!—they each thought about and felt what they could do to help *the other*. They were simultaneously working as individuals *and* as social creatures.

This is in accordance with and also emphasizes the tenets of REBT, which holds that individuals exist in their own unique right *and* as part of their social group. Both individualism and sociability seem to be innate and necessary for human survival. Both are also encouraged by social learning—though to different degrees in varying cultures. Jan and Ed came to therapy to increase their personal happiness—and to function more happily together. REBT often first gets around to their *individual* problems and solutions—so that they can communicate better *together*.

The third exercise Harper presented to Ed and Jan was for them to ask themselves and to discuss with each other: "How can we make life more interesting and enjoyable?" Harper, of course, implies interesting and enjoyable *together*. But, once again, don't they both *individually* have to do the enjoying? One would hope so!

A number of psychologists—such as Edward Sampson and Kenneth Gergen—have recently pointed out the dangers and limitations of our Western concepts of individualism and the advantages of some Eastern cultures' greater stresses on social sacrifice. They make a good point. But cultures that train their members to put others first and themselves second have to orient themselves toward *enjoying* this group outlook. And doesn't that include their individually enjoying it?

Ed and Jan were given REBT homework exercises. How about giving yourself some exercises to help you use the lessons included in this chapter? As noted, even making your and your partner's life more interesting and enjoyable takes thinking, problem-solving, discussing, planning, experimenting, rethinking, rediscussing, replanning, and re-experimenting. As Harper observed to Jan and Ed, "this is hard work, not a quick fix." So is mating in general!

Let us now do some exercises to help you increase your frustration tolerance and prepare you for the hard work that is required for successful mating.

Sample Exercise 5A: Making Myself Aware of My Low Frustration Tolerance (LFT) in Aspects of Dating, Relating, and Mating and My Irrational Beliefs (IBs) That Encourage My LFT

Occasions on Which I Avoided Doing What Was Beneficial or Did What Was Harmful to Me

IBs That Encouraged Me to Avoid Doing What Was Beneficial or Do What Was Harmful To Me

Spent money I could not afford to spend, knowing it would upset my partner.

I *absolutely need* the things this money will buy even though I cannot afford them. I *can't stand* being deprived and not getting what I strongly desire.

Criticized my partner severely even though I knew s/he couldn't take my criticism. Told myself to shut my big mouth but stupidly opened it and let my partner have it.

My partner is acting foolishly and I *have to* correct her/him. I *can't bear* keeping my feelings in. It's *awful* to have to shut up when I'm right about this. I *must* get my partner to change!

Refused to go out of my way to satisfy my partner's needs for more affection and sex.

I *shouldn't have to be* more affectionate and sexually involved when I don't feel like being so. It's *too* hard to push myself like this! I'm *unable* to give more than I am now giving. My partner is unfair and is no damned good for demanding more than I naturally feel like giving!

Didn't help my partner keep our apartment clean and tidy. Only helped him/her on a few occasions when I really felt like doing so and found it easy to cooperate.

My partner is too finicky and demanding—as s/he *shouldn't* be! Why should I have to work so hard and do so many unpleasant things? It's unfair! Life is too short to do the things my partner wants me to do. I never did them when I lived by myself, so I shouldn't have to do them now!

Exercise 5A (cont.)

Occasions on Which I Avoided Doing What Was Beneficial or Did What Was Harmful to Me	IBs That Encouraged Me to Avoid Doing What Was Beneficial or Do What Was Harmful To Me
Kept breaking appointments with my partner and coming late when I did keep them.	I *must* do exactly what I want to do first—before I keep my appointments with my partner and before I leave early to show up on time. I have *too much* to do, and since my partner will forgive me, I'll take care of myself first and put him/her second. Time should stretch and allow me to do everything I feel like doing before I keep my appointments with my partner. I need the love and favors I get from my partner but following his or her rules about appointments is too rough, and I *can't* do it!
Kept avoiding seeing my partner's relatives and was often nasty to them even when my partner felt very upset about this.	I didn't marry my partner's damned relatives and s/he should understand this! They're stupid and obnoxious—and deserve my boycotting them and telling them off! My partner is very inconsiderate when s/he makes me visit boring relatives. S/he should be wise enough to boycott them, too!
Kept overeating in spite of my poor health and my partner's upsetness about my self-defeating food intake.	I can get away with it! I can keep eating and not ruin my health. My partner *should* leave me alone and *must* stop nagging me about my eating. S/he is after me too much and I can't tolerate that! Eating is the main pleasure I have, and I must not be deprived of good food. How *horrible* it is to be deprived!

Exercise 5A

Occasions on Which I Avoided Doing What Was Beneficial or Did What Was Harmful to Me	IBs That Encouraged Me to Avoid Doing What Was Beneficial or Do What Was Harmful To Me
_____	_____
_____	_____
_____	_____
_____	_____
_____	_____
_____	_____
_____	_____
_____	_____
_____	_____
_____	_____
_____	_____
_____	_____
_____	_____
_____	_____
_____	_____
_____	_____
_____	_____

Sample Exercise 5B: Disputing My Irrational Beliefs (IBs) That Encourage My Low Frustration Tolerance (LFT)

IBs That Encourage Me to Avoid Doing What Is Beneficial or to Do What Is Harmful to Me	Disputing My IBs and Coming Up With RBs That Will Help Me Reduce My Low Frustration Tolerance (LFT)
I *absolutely need* the things this money will buy even though I cannot afford them. I *can't stand* being deprived now and not getting what I strongly desire.	*Dispute:* Why do I *absolutely need* the things that money will buy even though I can't afford them? *Answer:* I *don't* need what I want in this respect! *Dispute:* Can I really not *stand* being deprived now and not getting what I strongly desire? *Answer:* Of course I can stand it and not die of deprivation! I can still find *much* happiness in other respects—and can arrange *later* pleasure by depriving myself *now*.
My partner is acting foolishly and I *have to* correct her/him. I *can't bear* keeping my feelings in. It's *awful* to have to shut up when I'm right about this. I *must* get my partner to change!	*Dispute:* Do I *have to* correct my partner if s/he is acting foolishly? *Answer:* Obviously not—though that would be great, *if* s/he were ready to listen. *Dispute:* Why can't I bear keeping my feelings in? *Answer:* Only because I exaggeratedly *believe* I can't bear it and because I *define* the inconvenience of doing so as *awful*—or as worse than it *should* be. *Dispute:* Does my being right about my partner's mistakes mean that I *must* get him/her to change? *Answer:* No! S/he can clearly be wrong and stay wrong—while I tactfully keep my mouth shut!

Exercise 5B (cont.)

IBs That Encourage Me to Avoid Doing What Is Beneficial or to Do What Is Harmful to Me	Disputing My IBs and Coming Up With RBs That Will Help Me Reduce My Low Frustration Tolerance (LFT)
I *shouldn't have to* be more affectionate and sexually involved when I don't feel like being so. It's *too* hard to push myself like this! I'm *unable* to give more than I am now giving. My partner is unfair and is no damned good for demanding more than I naturally feel like giving!	*Dispute:* I *preferably* shouldn't have to be more affectionately and sexually involved with my partner when I don't feel like being so. But is it true that my preference *absolutely has* to be fulfilled? *Answer:* No—only if I choose to alienate and probably lose my partner. My preferences and desires don't *have to* be realized. *Dispute:* Am I really unable to give more love and sex than I am now giving? *Answer:* Yes, if I *make* myself unable. Otherwise, I *can* give more. *Dispute:* Is my partner unfair and no damned good for demanding more affection and sex than I naturally feel like giving? *Answer:* No! Aren't *I* unfair for withholding what I can give and what will probably make our relationship better?
My partner is too finicky and demanding—as s/he *shouldn't* be! Why should I have to work so hard and do so many unpleasant things? It's unfair! Life is too short to do the things my partner wants me to do. I never did them when I lived by myself, so I shouldn't have to do them now!	*Dispute:* Why is my partner *too* finicky and demanding about my not helping keep our apartment clean? *Answer:* S/he may really be finicky but my belief about his/her being *too* finicky goes with my demand that s/he *must not* be that demanding. But s/he *must* be that finicky if he or she *is.* Too bad! But I'd better realistically accept this finickiness if I

Exercise 5B (cont.)

IBs That Encourage Me to Avoid Doing What Is Beneficial or to Do What Is Harmful to Me	Disputing My IBs and Coming Up With RBs That Will Help Me Reduce My Low Frustration Tolerance (LFT)

choose to stay with this partner. *Dispute:* Is it really *unfair* that I have to work so hard to do so many unpleasant things to please my partner? *Answer:* No, it is painful, but not necessarily unfair. Even if it is unfair, I'd better do those things—or else calmly leave my partner. *Dispute:* Does it follow that because I never kept my apartment clean and tidy when I lived by myself, I shouldn't have to do so now? *Answer:* No, it doesn't follow at all! In this new relationship I'd better do many things that I never did before.

I *must do* exactly what I want to do first—before I keep my appointments with my partner and before I leave early to show up on time. I have *too much* to do, and since my partner will forgive me, I'll take care of myself first and put him/her second. Time should stretch and allow me to do everything I feel like doing before I keep my appointments with my partner. I need the love and favors I get from my partner but following his or her rules about appointments is too rough, and I *can't* do it!

Dispute: Where will it get me if I think I must do exactly what I want before I keep my appointments with my partner and before I leave early to show up on time? *Answer:* (1) Partnerless! (2) Remaining the procrastinating baby that I am! *Dispute:* Do I really have *too much* to do before I get out on time to be early for my appointments with my partner? *Answer:* No—much but not *too much* to do. Some of it I can *not* do—or sensibly can do later. *Dispute:* Should time stretch and allow me to do everything I want to do so that I can keep my ap-

COMMUNICATING AND PROBLEM-SOLVING AS A COUPLE

Exercise 5B (cont.)

IBs That Encourage Me to Avoid Doing What Is Beneficial or to Do What Is Harmful to Me	Disputing My IBs and Coming Up With RBs That Will Help Me Reduce My Low Frustration Tolerance (LFT)
	pointments on time with my partner? *Answer:* Like hell it should! It won't. *Dispute:* Is it true that I *can't* follow my partner's rules and thereby win his/her favor that I need? *Answer:* Can't? What drivel! I foolishly *won't.* I don't *need* his/her love and favors but prefer them. So I'd better push myself.
I didn't marry my partner's damned relatives and s/he should understand this! They're stupid and obnoxious—and deserve my boycotting them and telling them off! My partner is very inconsiderate when s/he makes me visit boring relatives. S/he should be wise enough to boycott them, too!	*Dispute: Must* my partner understand that I didn't marry his/her damned relatives and therefore never try to get me to see them? *Answer:* Lots of luck! To some extent his/her relatives go with my marriage ride. Visiting them will hardly kill me! *Dispute:* Are his/her relatives really *that* stupid and obnoxious? *Answer:* Only to my prejudiced view. Even if they are, they hardly deserve my boycotting them and telling them off. That won't make them less stupid and less obnoxious! *Dispute:* Is my partner really inconsiderate of me when s/he makes me visit his/her boring relatives? *Answer:* No, s/he is merely following his/her own bent and asking me to help him/her follow it. My partner *should* stick with his/

Exercise 5B (cont.)

IBs That Encourage Me to Avoid Doing What Is Beneficial or to Do What Is Harmful to Me	Disputing My IBs and Coming Up With RBs That Will Help Me Reduce My Low Frustration Tolerance (LFT)
	her boring relatives—and even enjoy them. We can't have *everything* in common—including this one.
I can get away with it! I can keep eating and not ruin my health. My partner *should* leave me alone and *must* stop nagging me about my eating. S/he is after me too much and I can't tolerate that! Eating is the main pleasure I have, and I must not be deprived of good food. How *horrible* to be deprived!	*Dispute:* Can I really get away with eating too much and not ruin my health? *Answer:* Very unlikely! I'd be quite an unusual exception to the rule. *Dispute:* Who says that my partner *must* stop nagging me about my eating? *Answer:* I say it—and I'll thereby make myself angry and help ruin our relationship. *Dispute:* Is my partner after me *too much?* Can I not tolerate his/her nagging? *Answer:* I *see* it as too much, but it's only much. Even if s/he does it much more than other partners would, it's mainly for my good. Maybe I'd better nag myself!

Exercise 5B

IBs That Encourage Me to Avoid Doing What Is Beneficial or Do What Is Harmful to Me	Disputing My IBs and Coming Up With RBs That Will Help Me Reduce My Low Frustration Tolerance (LFT)

Sample Exercise 5C: Tasks That I Can Make Myself Uncomfortably Do to Reduce My Low Frustration Tolerance (LFT)

Tasks That I Can Make Myself Uncomfortably Do to Reduce My Low Frustration Tolerance (LFT)	Rational Coping Self-Statements I Can Use to Help Myself Do These Uncomfortable Tasks
Speak up when I am afraid to be criticized by my partner or others.	If I don't force myself to speak up, I will *increase* my fear of doing so. I will train myself to speak up *less* and may sabotage our open and honest relationship.
Go for a date with a potential partner who I feel will reject me.	I have less to lose by being rejected than by not going at all. I can learn by going on the date even if it turns out badly. Rejection doesn't make *me* bad.
Take a trip to a foreign country alone.	It won't kill me to be alone. I can learn to be more self-sufficient. If I get into any difficulty it will only be inconvenient, hardly the end of the world.
Exercise regularly, though I hate to do so.	It will give me good health benefits. The pain of the exercise will be brief—the pain of not doing it may last forever!
Eat much less delicious food than I prefer to eat.	The pleasure of eating will be brief—but the pain of overeating may be long! I will enjoy the fact that I am so disciplined! I will set a good example for my partner.
Stay with a partner who is often nasty and critical when leaving this partner would be inconvenient.	I cannot enjoy my partner's nastiness but can enjoy not taking it too seriously. I can stay, without getting upset, until it is much less inconvenient to leave.

Exercise 5C (cont.)

Tasks That I Can Make Myself Uncomfortably Do to Reduce My Low Frustration Tolerance (LFT)	Rational Coping Self-Statements I Can Use to Help Myself Do These Uncomfortable Tasks
Shut my big mouth when tempted to tell my partner off.	The pleasure of telling my partner off isn't worth the pain that will almost certainly follow my doing so. I can do myself a lot of good by shutting my mouth, staying for the present, and refusing to upset myself about my partner's actions.
Force myself to help my partner when I think that s/he is demanding that I do a foolish act.	The help I give my partner won't take too long while his/her displeasure and anger if I don't give it may last forever! I can actually enjoy the pleasure of satisfying my partner even though I don't like this way of satisfying him/her.
Agree to go along with my partner's foolish expenditures when we could use the money to much better advantage.	Even though I agree to spend foolishly with my partner, I can improve our relationship. Perhaps I can show him/her *later* how foolish our expenditures were. Even when we spend money on foolish things, I can often manage to enjoy these things.

Exercise 5C

Tasks That I Can Make Myself Uncomfortably Do to Reduce My Low Frustration Tolerance (LFT)	Rational Coping Self-Statements I Can Use to Help Myself Do These Uncomfortable Tasks

6

Better Sex for Better Couplehood

When we wrote *A Guide to a Successful Marriage*, the sixties were just beginning. Although both of us already were "established" experts on SMF (sex/marriage/family) matters, we were nevertheless rebels against the establishment and tried to communicate a much more liberal and democratic attitude toward SMF than prevailed at the time. But times have changed. In some ways, only the Far Right (now a "moral *minority*") sound the way almost everybody did in 1961. But the culture has not changed so much that people who want a liberal and democratic SMF environment can relax and feel utopia is just around the corner.

Our use of REBT from 1955 onward made us aware of several important aspects of sex therapy: (1) sexual problems are usually bound up with nonsexual problems; (2) partners can themselves check on whether each are making therapy gains; (3) each partner can help the other to learn and to use REBT principles; (4) REBT, especially through homework exercises that couples undertake, provides problem-solving methods and experience. Therapy itself becomes an effective coping experience.

While it is important for therapists to teach specialized sex techniques and skills to their clients, they should also help these clients to become adept at *human* relations. REBT, though hardly neglecting sexual coping, concentrates on teaching *general* relationship methods.

When we use REBT with couples sex therapy, the couples provide a fine source of information about their own interactions, and give us a steady workshop situation in which we (and they) test out and improve upon problem-solving skills developed in the therapy hours. Soon, if all goes well, the couple will work things out on their own, using the knowledge and skills learned in therapy.

Does this mean neglecting the methods of treating tough sex problems that we and other sex therapists—such as Masters and Johnson, Joseph LoPicollo, Helen Kaplan, Lonnie Barbach, and Bernie Zilbergeld—have developed over the last several decades? Of course not. But we now more clearly see sex problems as part of general emotional difficulties and as being interactional as well as individual. So we treat sex issues rationally, emotively, and behaviorally, just as we treat *other* problems that commonly—and, often *more* than commonly—arise in human interactions.

To illustrate applying REBT to sexual adjustment in couples, let us return to Jan and Ed. Here are some excerpts from their sixth therapy session.

Jan: Hey, we've been doing great on all this problem-solving stuff—I mean really great! But maybe the price is too high. This guy used to be all over me, and I loved it. Now we do sex by the numbers, and we both look and act bored. What price are we paying for all this rationality?

R.A.H.: Yes, but you and Ed remember that exercise three, which we mentioned before, includes efforts to make life ever more interesting and enjoyable. Rationality helps you overcome problems, but is not an end in itself—and certainly not a substitute for sex enjoyment. In using REBT, we approach sex problems in essentially the same way as other difficulties. You two reported no sex problem before, but Jan says that you now have less sex interest and enthusiasm. Do you agree, Ed? (He did.) Okay, we don't require exercises one and two, but let's go into exercise three again, which you both have used before. (They closed their eyes, and each focused on how they could change their own behavior to make sex fun.)

Ed: This is a tough one because I think it has some paradoxes. I can think of ways to change my ways of thinking, feeling, perceiving, and acting that would probably have us panting hot, but I think I'd be a phony. And *that's* no route to long-term interest and enjoyment. But, on the other hand, I am still interested in Jan sexually as well as in several other ways.

Jan: Well, I came up with one particularly desirable behavior change on my part. After four or five really great weeks, these past few days I've been thinking, "How come you ain't hot for luscious me, man?" And I've been taking it very personally that Ed clearly wasn't. But I just realized now that I can't honestly change my *perception* of what is going on. Because Ed isn't all over me all the time may mean that he has more respect for me as a person, as an equal, which is what I was screaming for not too damned many weeks ago. Also, because I'm now more interested in Ed in a lot of other ways than as a stud, I am probably sending out fewer Cleopatra-is-ready-to-be-laid flashes and scents.

Ed: Yeah, what Jan has just said fits in with what I was going on to say. My growing interest in Jan as a person seems to interfere somewhat with my interest in her as a great lay—not easy lay, Jan, but *great* lay. And I do still think and feel that way. It was probably the things she said about seeing her more as a person than as a sex object.

R.A.H.: I think I can help here. First of all, I think you have both developed anxiety about your reduced sex interest. Being alarmed and being also very devoted to the REBT program of making life more interesting and enjoyable, you have self-consciously forced yourselves (by the numbers, as Jan said) to each show yourself and the other one how overwhelmingly passionate you were. Whenever you try too hard—because you think you *absolutely must* succeed, let's say, at table tennis—you create anxiety that is likely to mess up your game. That goes many times over for sex, which is easily inhibited by anxiety. Let me make some points that may be helpful.

First, it is usual and normal for people when they are concentrating on a number of other things—in your case, on making some difficult behavior changes—to have their libidos temporarily wane. Second, it is also common for them—especially those who have never had sexual problems—to panic if a problem suddenly arises. Third, you are now well equipped with REBT procedures to apply to this new situation, as you already have done in your experiences with exercise two. One REBT response that I'd like to remind you of is that it wouldn't be terrible, awful, and catastrophic *even* if sex for the two of you became somewhat less exciting than in the past. You do have, as you both have indicated, increasing interest and enjoyment in many other aspects of your life. So you probably *won't* have less enjoyable sex. But even if you *do*, things will not be terrible. To summarize: relax, and your sex problem may already be on the wane.

Suppose Ed and Jan had had a *real* sex problem, what could we, as REBT therapists, do to help them with it? Actually, their problem *was* quite real and, like most sex (and non-sex) problems derived from anxiety or from *must*urbating about the *necessity* of success. Their anxiety deepened as they thought they *had* to please and be totally loved by the other partner and this anxiety led to hurt and suspicion. Partly, though, because Jan brought it up quite soon in therapy and partly because both Ed and Jan were already experienced in REBT couple exercises, their sex problem was so quickly dealt with that it seemed almost "unreal." Using exercise three for the next few weeks, they focused on how they could change their own behavior so that each of them could have more sex fun. Jan focused on being more sexy in her dress, her scent, and in her verbal and gestural approaches to Ed. She also used imagery to recall how sexually exciting he was when they first met and helped herself experience quicker and more intense orgasms. Ed also actively took the challenge of focusing on Jan's whole body, instead of mainly her genitals, when they were having sex, and of giving himself and her increased sensual pleasures even when his orgasms were not intense. He made sure that he—and Jan—had more prolonged sensual enjoyment even when their sexual peaks were quick and short. He became so focused on this aspect of their sexuality that other aspects were much less boring. Jan pushed herself to focus on bodily sensitivity, too; and they both resonated to the challenge of doing so. Even on some nights when they were not sexually aroused to begin with, they ultimately became so and enjoyed their own now-enhanced sensuality.

When couples have a sex problem that is more complicated, less readily defined, more long-standing, and apparently deep-seated, REBT couple procedures are similar. Exercise one (in which they make sure they understand each other's view of the problem) may require more work in both therapy sessions and in homework assignments, instead of being quickly resolved, as happened in Jan and Ed's case. Exercise two (focusing on how each partner can change to make things better) may only be done slowly and with small advances. Exercise three (what we can both do to enjoy our relationship more) may be tougher for one or both partners but can also be a rewarding experience.

Sex compatibility in mating is not always solved, as in Ed and Jan's case, by love. Many couples—like Sid and Jo who I (Dr. Ellis) wrote about in chapter two—love each other, all right, but really *are* somewhat sexually incompatible, in which case their sex problems may erode their love.

Sex differences in couples arise for a number of reasons. For example:

1. One partner—as in Jo's case—may be relatively low-sexed and the other—as was true of Sid—relatively high-sexed. Jo really wanted sex *a maximum* of once a month and Sid wanted it a *minimum* of once a week. No great compatibility!

Possible solution: The low-sexed partner finds some sexually uninvolved, noncoital way of satisfying the high-sexed partner. Thus s/he can do so with his/her mouth, tongue, vibrator, or in some other manner, while remaining unsexy but loving and interested in the other's satisfaction. One client I saw, who enjoyed intercourse about once a month, massaged her husband's penis with her large breasts twice a week and gave him "stupendous" orgasms—which she immensely enjoyed his having.

2. One partner, for various physical reasons—such as physical impotence, pain, or severe back pain—may not be able to have some forms of "normal" penile-vaginal intercourse.

Possible solution: Again, the penile-vaginally handicapped partner may use his/her other body appendages or orifices to satisfy the other partner. One husband who had painful intercourse because of sores on his penis, and whose wife was vaginally sensitive and greatly enjoyed intromission, brought her to terrific orgasms with his fingers vigorously massaging her vagina. A wife who had dyspareunia (pain during vaginal intercourse), let her husband have anal intercourse with her, and, after a while, she began to enjoy it.

3. Some partners, for various neurotic reasons, are phobic about certain kinds of sex. One of my (Dr. Ellis') woman friends could have five or ten orgasms a night through clitoral manipulation but never overcame the trauma of her being raped by her uncle when she was fifteen, and always suffered great pain during intercourse. When I dated her I was easily able to give her powerful orgasms by manipulating her clitoral region while passionately kissing her breasts. I went with her for a full year and we never had intercourse at all but she insisted I was by far the best of the five lovers she had up to that time. Since she was fully creative and talented with her fingers, I found that she was one of the very best lovers that I had had, too!

4. Some partners take twenty or thirty minutes to come to orgasm in intercourse, while their mate may not be able to last that long or may experience pain when he or she has prolonged coitus.

Possible solution: One woman who took almost an hour to come during intercourse while her mate took only a minute or two arranged to have him copulate with her and come after a short while, then he used a vibrator to give her orgasms in ten or more minutes.

5. One partner may require fetishistic sex acts—like being tied up and beaten—which the other may not enjoy.

Possible solutions: The partner who doesn't enjoy the fetishistic acts can tolerate participating in them once in a while, providing that they have "regular" sex most of the time. Or, in return for engaging in the fetishistic act, s/he can receive some special kind of sexual or nonsexual enjoyment from the other partner. One man who didn't like vigorously pinching his wife's behind—which brought her to terrific orgasms—arranged with her to give in to his own fetish: having her masturbate him while viewing a sexy movie and risking letting the other movie-goers see what they were doing.

6. One mate may be quite monogamous while the other achieves great enjoyment from having multiple sex partners and even simultaneous ones.

Possible solution: The nonmonogamous mate may work on his/her frustration tolerance and bear up with the "horrors" of being sexually restricted to the other partner while enjoying the other aspects of their relationship. Or, as in the case of one of my clients, a man who was only interested in having sex with his wife while she wanted to have sex with her ex-husband, too, he worked out an agreement with her. Rather than lose her, he agreed to let her spend one night a month with her ex-husband as long as she agreed afterward to do anything he wanted sexually, and sometimes what he wanted nonsexually, during the rest of the month. Both of them accepted the disadvantages of this arrangement for two years, until she decided to give up her ex-husband as an additional lover.

For various reasons, mates can warmly care for each other and have little sex compatibility. Conversely, I (A.E.) have also seen a good many couples who are only compatible sexually but in practically no other way. Even after they get divorced, they sometimes get together regularly just because they enjoy sex together!

Not every sexually incompatible couple is able to work out suitable arrangements whereby both of them are satisfied in bed; and many stay together, and have quite good marriages, in spite of having little or no sex with each other for a good number of years. Defining sex only as intercourse is a serious mistake for many couples. Indeed, where one partner—either the man or the woman—insists that coitus is the only form of sex that he or she will tolerate, serious breakdown in the couple's sex participation often occurs.

Dr. Harper and I, therefore, quickly and frankly show many of our clients that sex equals sex rather than equals mere intercourse; and that there are many kinds of coital and non-coital relations they can participate in with each other when one or both of them dislike regular intercourse.

Duties, of course, can sometimes be enjoyable—such as one's duty to be helpful to one's children—and enjoyments can also be made into duties. Sex duties and sex enjoyments, therefore, are not always incompatible. Freedom and democracy in bed, however, are as good as they are out of bed. So if you and your partner will give yourself the leeway to experiment sexually, to do largely what you *want* to do and not just what you think it is your *duty* to do, and if you both will avoid turning your sex enjoyments into invariable duties, you will be following the REBT concepts of removing your needless blocks and neuroses *and* living your relationship as fully and enjoyably as you both are capable of doing.

EXERCISES FOR CHAPTER 6

As we have indicated in this chapter, sex problems almost always stem from general emotional problems rather than—as Freud wrongly thought—emotional disturbances being caused by sex difficulties. Even when sexual neuroses *seem* to start things going, they almost always have at bottom the two main issues that we have been steadily seeing throughout this book: (1) self-downing; and (2) low frustration tolerance and anger.

Take, for example, Freud's famous Oedipus or Electra complex. When I (Dr. Ellis) practiced psychoanalysis, I looked for this complex and rarely found it. In a few instances, I discovered that my clients' fathers were quite jealous of their sons' attachments to their mothers, showed rage against them, and helped these sons to be afraid of having sex with women. But the vast majority of my clients who had jealous fathers were not afraid of being castrated, were quite potent with women, and often had reasonably good relationships with their partners.

Those few males I saw as clients who were afraid of being punished by other males for having sex with women were almost always putting themselves down for not being able to compete against "better" men and were telling themselves that vying for female partners was harder than it *should* be—therefore copping out of trying to win the favors of women.

I have seen relatively few males over the past fifty years who were guilty about lusting after their mothers (or sisters) and who therefore couldn't function well with female sex partners. They almost always hated themselves for doing the "wrong" thing and, as self-downers, felt undeserving and worthless. Whether or not their fathers were jealous of them was usually irrelevant.

Of all the thousands of people with sex problems that we both have seen over the years, practically all of them felt inadequate sexually because they strongly believed that they *should* be more competent than they actually were. In addition, many of them knew that they would have to make certain adjustments or changes to have satisfactory sex with a given partner—that is, do what their partner wanted sexually or nonsexually—but they found it "too hard" to do so, felt that it *shouldn't* be that hard, and therefore refused to arrange to get the satisfaction that they wanted.

So there we go again! If you or your mate are having a rough time sexually, by all means get help and find out what is blocking you. A little useful information may solve your problems. But look, also, for the possible self-downing and low frustration tolerance that may well be creating your problem. If you find either or both of these, here are some exercises you can use to reduce these disturbances.

Sample Exercise 6A: Discovering My IBs That May Be Involved With My Sex Problems

My Sex Problem With My Partner Is . . .	My IBs That Lead to or Stem From This Problem May Possibly Be . . .
Low sex desire for my partner.	I *shouldn't* have to do anything to arouse myself with my partner. My partner must always want sex exactly when I want it and must go out of his/her way to satisfy me. I should always be greatly aroused by my partner and there's something very wrong with me if I am not. Maybe I don't really love my partner.
Very high sex desire for my partner when my partner has less desire.	There must be something wrong with me. If I loved my partner more, I wouldn't keep plaguing him/her for more sex. My partner should be much more desirous of me than s/he is!
I take too long to have an orgasm.	I shouldn't take so long. I must be seriously deficient! My partner will hate me for taking so long!
Having orgasms rarely or not at all.	If I don't have an orgasm that will be terrible! I'm obviously no good at sex. Arranging to have an orgasm takes too much work!
Having trouble succeeding in or enjoying intercourse.	I must have great intercourse to be good in bed! Intercourse is the *only* right way to enjoy sex with my partner. If I can't satisfy my partner in intercourse I'm not a real man or a real woman.

Exercise 6A (cont.)

My Sex Problem With My Partner Is . . .	My IBs That Lead to or Stem From This Problem May Possibly Be . . .
Strongly desiring kinky sex.	I shouldn't have these kinky desires! I'm abnormal! If I engage in kinky sex I'm an evil person!
My partner doesn't have an orgasm when we have intercourse.	There's something wrong with me! I should be able to make him or her come during intercourse. I'm a failure!
I can't last in sex and come to orgasm too rapidly.	Oh, my God, this is awful! I'm just no good at sex and will never be! Normal people last longer—so I should, too!

Exercise 6A

My Sex Problem With My Partner Is . . .	My IBs That Lead to or Stem From This Problem May Possibly Be . . .
_____	_____
_____	_____
_____	_____
_____	_____
_____	_____
_____	_____
_____	_____
_____	_____
_____	_____
_____	_____
_____	_____
_____	_____
_____	_____
_____	_____
_____	_____

Sample Exercise 6B: Rational Coping Statements I Can Use If I Have Sex Problems With My Partner

Rational Coping Self-Statements I Can Use If I Have Sex Problems With My Partner

Even though my partner and I love each other, we differ in important ways and may not always enjoy sex at the same time together.

If my partner is more highly or more lowly sexed than I am, we can make adjustments and still usually satisfy each other.

I would *prefer* to have strong orgasms and to achieve them fairly quickly, but I don't *have to* do so.

I would prefer to be able to give my partner strong orgasms fairly quickly, but if this is not possible, we can still enjoy sex and satisfy each other.

If my partner or I have sex problems, this is not shameful. We can openly talk about them and cooperatively do our best to solve them.

If my sex life with my partner is not easily and spontaneously great, we can work at finding ways to improve it.

Kinky sex is not bad or evil as long as we mutually enjoy it and do not physically harm ourselves.

If either my partner or I comes to orgasm very rapidly, we can work at slowing down and can find various ways, and not necessarily intercourse, in which to enjoy ourselves.

Even if my partner and I never have a great sex life, we can still love each other and enjoy a fine relationship.

Exercise 6B

Rational Coping Self-Statements I Can Use If I Have Sex Problems
With My Partner

_____

_____

_____

_____

_____

_____

_____

_____

_____

_____

_____

_____

_____

_____

_____

Sample Exercise 6C: Things I Can Do to Increase My Low Frustration Tolerance If My Partner and I Have Sex Problems

Things I Can Do to Increase My Low Frustration Tolerance About My Sex Relations With My Partner

Be patient with my partner and explore her or his sex problems or dissat-
isfactions.

Show my partner what my sex preferences are but not demand that he or
she fulfill them.

Discuss my and my partner's sex differences and work out some compromises when our differences remain.

If necessary for a better relationship with my partner, live with my sex
frustration and work at improving our nonsexual lives.

Get some sex training so that I can satisfy my partner more in the ways he
or she would like to be satisfied.

Try some new sex techniques with my partner when the usual ones are
satisfying to me but not to her or him.

When I am sexually deprived with my partner, strongly convince myself
that this is only inconvenient, not *awful*, and that we can still have an
enjoyable relationship.

Exercise 6C

Things I Can Do to Increase My Low Frustration Tolerance About
My Sex Relations With My Partner
_____

_____

_____

_____

_____

_____

_____

_____

_____

_____

_____

_____

_____

7

Saving Time and Money and Enjoying Life More

When we first began our research, teaching, writing, and counseling about human relations, people were greatly concerned and often disturbed about sex. But even now that people's sex problems are talked and written about more openly, difficulties among couples have hardly disappeared. However, today's social environment gives a couple (married, unmarried, homosexual, heterosexual, ethnically the same or different) a better chance than in the past to work out ways of relating to each other.

This is not exactly true in economic affairs. The road is often limited and the hard-won freedom open to a couple in working out a satisfactory sex life is often not available in matters of money and leisure. Although social myth and personal fantasy are still rife ("You can make anything you want of yourself"), most *individuals* have restricted choice as to how to earn a living, how much money they will save from that earning process, and how much time and resources will be left for leisure-time activities.

When it comes to *couples*, things are often worse. First, even the individuals who once had a career choice have often already exercised that choice and are now highly restricted. Second, those who have not already made a career choice often have meager financial resources. Third, their communities often offer little help in working out financial problems.

How does REBT enter this rough scene to help couples? Mainly by showing them how to accept the "grim" realities of work and income, while not being too pessimistic and not cavalierly running away from them. Thus, if couples still believe in the great myths of rugged individualism and a chicken in every pot, they can be shown that today's world often mandates both partners working, sharing the responsibilities of child rearing, coping with the unleisurely tasks of shopping, cleaning, and paying bills. Also, because both partners may work and have children to care for, they may have increased expenses (such as two cars or commutes to work) and less time for being intimate and leisurely, which means they may have more practical problems to solve in their partnerships.

Let us look again at an actual couple with some of these problems. Here is how I (Dr. Harper) used REBT to work with them.

Ron: We have really been approaching this relationship quite intelligently, Bill and I both think. It's the first time I've lived with anyone, but Bill has been married before.

Bill: For a couple of years. But fortunately no kids and even more fortunately, no real fuss from my wife when I decided to stop forcing myself to pretend I was really straight. I was too scared of AIDS to do any messing around in gay places. Then I met Ron and we took HIV tests and came out clean (he'd been afraid of messing around, too, with a few exceptions, where he was just plain lucky).

Ron: So, as I was saying, we think we have worked things out pretty well. We had separately done some REBT reading and listening to tapes. So we did some more and then decided we would try living together. We have some trouble with families, friends, neighbors, and, in Bill's case, an employer. You know, "Hey, you guys can't do this dreadful thing of living together and going around together. It's degradation and degeneration, and so forth." But everybody, with the exception of Bill's employer, got used to the idea.

Bill: I ended up getting fired, but I got a better job almost immediately. Better, that is, in money, but worse in the time and energy it takes to make the better income. I could probably get even more money by suing my original employer (a conservative lawyer tells me I have a splendid case). But money isn't really our problem. And sex isn't our problem. I always heard that if it isn't money, it's sex; and if it isn't sex, it's money. But with us it's neither. Time is our problem. Time to enjoy ourselves. Time to enjoy our relationship. Time to live.

Ron: Don't wax too wildly poetic, Bill, or Doc will think all our problems come from being gay. In fact, we get that almost all the time from people who know us. They seem to say, "Hey, what have a couple of queers like you got to complain about?" This implies that only a red-blooded all-American heterosexual couple have the stern moral fiber needed to have a happy relationship. Even Bill has occasionally looked for some psychoanalytic crap about our deep-seated guilty feelings about being gay preventing our getting full satisfaction from our life together.

RAH: I see Bill ready to dispute that. But please let me intervene here. Your time problem is often basic to contemporary American life. It is shared to some degree by many of us. It may get more exaggerated by special factors (such as one's sexual orientation), but it is still often the same problem. The time problem is not quite as free of money problems as I think Bill was perhaps suggesting. If you have plenty of money, you can usually buy a lot of time; and if you have little money, a lot of time often won't lead to enjoyment. And—regarding your so-called deep-seated feelings of guilt—it is more likely that because you are not enjoying yourselves, you look for and find guilt feelings about being gay (a convenient hook on which you hang your nonenjoyment). You may indeed have some other problems associated with your homosexuality, but let's view this problem of time-to-enjoy-yourselves in its own right.

Enjoying yourself involves, one, learning to function efficiently, and two, learning what is fun for you and helpful to your social group. To do so, you had better also learn to engage in *tasks* with efficiency and zest. Try not to spend money and time without providing much enjoyment in the process. REBT's answer is to have us examine what we are doing in terms of how *efficiently* and *enjoyably* we are doing it.

Ron: On the efficiency thing, we've done some work. For example, we make out a supermarket list in advance, based on the next week's planned dinners and lunches, and we fairly and efficiently divide up household chores. We have a schedule of these chores posted in the kitchen. But proceeding efficiently doesn't make for fun—we find it all a pain in the ass.

R.A.H.: You're already ahead of many couples, however, in trying to organize your tasks. Many people balk at even the thought of carefully planning the use of either their time or their money. For most of us, whether we like spending a month scaling the Himalayas or a day at the beach, we work it out better by planning it in terms of both time and money issues.

Bill: Yeah, but there you hit it, man: *work.* We work our asses off in our respective jobs. We work out ways of keeping the damned home fires burning. We work out a schedule in time and money to include dry cleaning, laundry, haircuts, and new clothes. We work at getting along with other people on our jobs and in the community, so they don't decide to hang us as a couple of homos. We work at our relationship and at REBT. There's plenty of work, Doc, but where is the good old fun? Right, rational Ronnie?

Ron: Right, benign basket-case Billy.

R.A.H.: Even Bill's recitation of your work woes, Ron, and your reply all indicate you have made even more progress than I first thought. You have not only made considerable headway in organizing your life together, but you show signs of beginning to accept this as a way of life and of beginning to be kind of lighthearted about it.

Ron: I think we have a way to go on the lighthearted bit, but even lightheartedness falls short of having a car load of fun, doesn't it?

R.A.H.: Yes, I'm afraid more work is indicated (both Bill and Ron groan)—work focused on how to get more fun out of work. You two are already well on your way. You have taken step one: facing the fact that modern couples had better organize themselves or they won't be able to cope and to begin to *act* on enjoying themselves. As I indicated before, many people have difficulty even facing step two: realizing that hard work is a permanent ongoing process—a way of life. As a human, you have to *get* organized, and then *stay* organized, which calls for ongoing problem-solving.

Many of us rebel at step two. We often think and feel that after step one, things must come easy—living peachy keen without any special effort on our part. We not only have this tendency built into us as humans, but we also reinforce it in each other as couples. We say to each other, "So we mowed the lawn and cleaned the bathroom. Why can't we just relax and take it easy the rest of our lives? I thought good people were supposed to live happily ever after."

You two, however, seem also to have pretty well accepted step two. As I think you might put it, "Tough shit, man! That's where life is at." It's okay to be pissed off that life is as life is, but it is foolish to let your annoyance with hassles interfere with your coping. So much for efficiency. Now we come to tough step three: enjoyment. Let's see how we can work better on that.

Ron: Sorry to interrupt, but it's all starting to sound academic and phony to me. In the real situation these three steps are all mixed in together, and we can't really tip-toe through step one and step two in order to be ready for step three, "enjoyment."

RAH: You are right. No tip-toeing! In our REBT procedures we first try to demonstrate to people some of the self-defeating ways they are now behaving. At the same time, we attempt to show them how to discover *and* actually experience greater happiness and self-actualization. We also encourage them to sustain and extend their efforts when something short of a fairy godmother change is achieved. Complications can and often do develop. Some people, for example, make fine progress in learning to enjoy life and then lapse into feeling miserable about doing so—because they were presumably "put here to do greater and more noble things than to enjoy life," such as uphold family honor, serve God and/or country, or be a "wonderful" parent. Fine, if that's what they really want. But not if it's what they think they *should* and *must* want.

Bill: Back to the REBT anti-shoulds and anti-musts. Right?

RAH: Yes, back to non-musturbating! So let me again stress the difficulties of getting yourself to see where you are, where you realistically want to go, and how you can rationally try to get there. By your dealing, as you might guess I would say, with your firmly entrenched hindrances to permanently incorporating the desirable changes you want. Then to go on to step three.

Ron: To even enjoy the *work* of self-fulfillment?

RAH: Exactly. Working for money, for mental health, or for anything else need *not* be as unenjoyable as you make it. You can find distinct satisfaction in your careers—by yourself and with your coworkers. Yes, you *can* find ways—by using your imagination and by experimenting—to make your work more enjoyable.

Bill: And our life as a couple, too? *Really* more enjoyable?

RAH: Yes—almost always, definitely yes.

Ron: In a word—how?

RAH: In quite a few words, by maximizing and using your leisure. But this, not so strangely enough, means first agreeing on and carrying out your responsibilities to yourself, to each other, and even to your social group—the group in which you *choose* to live. Whether you like it or not, your couple life (like that of most people) is filled with obligations. Whether you call them "duties" or not, these obligations add to your work in leaving you little time when you are utterly "free." Damned little leisure! But, of course, this leisure time gives you more choice about when and how you will enjoy yourself.

Ron: I think I see your point. Are you saying that if we work on an *efficient* scheduling of our obligations and *determine* we are going to have fun in fulfilling this schedule that our life as a couple will become a ball?

RAH: Not entirely, of course. But you and Bill do have some degree of choice about what social obligations you will fulfill, and how efficiently you will go about carrying them out. If you choose sensibly, you can do more *un*obligated tasks together and separately. But, again, you have to *strive* to do this.

Bill: Too bad, as you often say in REBT. But I don't think that will turn us off. Although we like to bitch a lot about it, we believe in working for more pleasure.

Ron: I think Bill speaks for me, too. Shall we take the homework assignment between now and our next session of analyzing our time together and devising some concrete plans for making it more efficient and enjoyable?

RAH: Fine! But make enjoyment your number-one priority. The most efficient way of doing something is not always the most enjoyable way. For example, for one of you to clean the kitchen while the other does the weeks' shopping might be more efficient than to shop together, but you might have more fun with the latter approach.

Bill: I see what you mean.

Ron: Yes, let's try.

In this chapter, we have taken a very brief and perhaps oversimplified look at the money/leisure situation in which many contemporary couples find themselves. We intentionally didn't try to deal with a multitude of serious social problems where, for example, money is insufficient and community resources are inadequate for even minimum health and decency standards and where couples lack almost all resources to enjoy themselves. Nor did we discuss couple relationships that are seriously hampered by alcohol, drugs, illness, or other factors. What we noted, however, was that even in "good" situations, couples can find themselves in a real time and money squeeze, and we concentrated on the time factor to show how REBT can help couples maximize leisure and thereby work for greater enjoyment.

EXERCISES FOR CHAPTER 7

Saving time and money involves developing your high frustration tolerance (HFT) and your unconditional self-acceptance (USA). So do most aspects of self-discipline! You—like other people—largely overspend because you think you *need* things you can't really afford and because you *must* show others that you are as affluent as they may be. And you may unrealistically save too much money because you think that you *can't* spend normally and that you *have* to save enormously to prove that your monetary worth equals your worth as a person.

REBT does stress financial sanity and Patricia Hunter and I (Dr. Ellis) wrote a whole book dedicated to REBT and money: *Why Am I Always Broke? How to Be Sane About Money.* The following exercises bring out some of the main points in that book—namely, how to save time and money to enjoy life more.

Sample Exercise 7A: Common Problems That My Partner and I May Have in Spending Time and Money and Enjoying Life More

Common Problems That My Partner and I May Have	IBs I May Create About This Problem	RBs That I Can Use to Alleviate This Problem
Inefficiently frittering away our time.	It's too hard to efficiently keep track of our time. I *shouldn't have to* do so! We can enjoy ourselves more if we only think of the pleasures of the moment. I *can't stand* taking the trouble to be more efficient.	Yes, it may be hard to efficiently keep track of our time, but it's hard*er* not to do so! We only have *one* life to live and enjoy—so we'd better plot, scheme, and push ourselves to enjoy it! The one thing we can never regain is lost time.
Griping when money is short—and still overspending.	It's *awful* to be short of money! My partner and I *must not* be deprived of things we really want! Other people have more money than we have and it's unfair that that they do. It shouldn't be so unfair!	It's highly inconvenient to be short of money, but it's hardly totally inconvenient or *awful*. My partner and I *must* be deprived of things we really want when we're short of money. Even if other people "unfairly" have more funds than we do, that unfairness has to exist when it does. Too bad!
Dealing with household problems as a team.	I hate boring housework and I *shouldn't* have to do it! My partner finds household tasks easier to do and s/he should therefore do more	No matter how much I hate housework I darned well better do it! Even though my partner finds it easier to do than I, I can do my share and enjoy

Exercise 7A (cont.)

Common Problems That My Partner and I May Have	IBs I May Create About This Problem	RBs That I Can Use to Alleviate This Problem
	than I. I'll wait to see if s/he gets going on them. Then maybe I'll pitch in, too. After all I do to please my partner sexually, s/he really should do most of the housework.	doing some of it as a team. I'll get going on it right away and serve as a model for my partner to follow. Just because I please my partner sexually and in other ways, there is no reason for me not to do my share of housework. This will thereby help us to avoid squabbles and aid our relationship.
Handling our children, especially when they are sick and difficult.	I'm no good at handling our children and therefore my partner should usually do so. I have too many other things to do, so s/he should mainly handle them. My partner *should* care for me very much and take most of the burden of handling the children off my hands.	If I'm not good as my partner at handling the children, I can learn to be better. Yes, I have many things to do, but so does my partner—let me be fair! Why should my partner care for me so much and take most of the burden of caring for the children off my hands? How about my showing him/her how much I care by doing my share of taking care of the burden of the children? Why can't I arrange

Exercise 7A (cont.)

Common Problems That My Partner and I May Have	IBs I May Create About This Problem	RBs That I Can Use to Alleviate This Problem
		for us to *enjoy* taking care of them together?
Budgeting and keeping our spending within the budget.	If there's anything I hate, it's budgeting, so I shouldn't have to do it! My partner foolishly exceeds our budget, so I might as well be lax, too. We made a mistake in arranging to pay so much rent, and now we have to skimp on everything. How awful! My partner should have stopped us from paying so much rent!	No matter how much I hate budgeting, my partner and I will get in much more financial trouble if we don't! Even though my partner foolishly exceeds our budget, I'd better help him/her stick to it and not be equally foolish! Yes, we made a mistake in arranging to pay so much rent, but it won't kill us to skimp on other things. Perhaps my partner should have stopped us from paying so much rent, but both of us *should* have kept us from making that mistake—fallible creatures that we are!
Severely criticizing my partner for his/her inefficiently wasting time, money, or perpetrating other kinds of disorganization.	My partner *should* be much more efficient! Because I am, s/he should darned well be. His/her inefficiency and wastefulness is ruining our lives! What a worth-	My partner has problems being more efficient and I'd better uncritically try to help him/her with them—or even make up for some of his/her wastefulness. It's

Exercise 7A (cont.)

Common Problems That My Partner and I May Have	IBs I May Create About This Problem	RBs That I Can Use to Alleviate This Problem
	less person s/he is!	good that I'm more efficient, but that never means s/he *must* be too. Her/his inefficiency is handicapping us but it's far from ruining our whole lives. S/he is acting badly in this respect, but s/he has many other good traits and is not a *bad person.*
Making little real effort to have fun and enjoyment with my partner.	It's *too much* trouble to *make* fun and *work for* enjoyment. This should come spontaneously and naturally. My partner must love me for *myself* and not because I amuse him/her or go out of my way to create enjoyment for him/her.	I may find it trouble to make fun and work for enjoyment with my partner, but it's not *too much* trouble. I can appreciably help our relationship. It need *not* come about spontaneously but may be better if planned There's no reason why my partner must love me for *myself* if I make no efforts to amuse him/her or go out of my way to create enjoyment for him/her. If I allow us to have a dull life, s/he will find me a dull person!

Exercise 7A

Common Problems That My Partner and I May Have	IBs I May Create About This Problem	RBs That I Can Use to Alleviate This Problem
Inefficiently frittering away our time		
Griping when money is short—and still overspending		
Dealing with household problems as a team		
Handling our children, especially when they are sick or difficult		
Budgeting and keeping our spending within the budget		
Severely criticizing my partner for his/her inefficiently wasting time, money, and perpetrating other kinds of disorganization		
Making little real effort to have fun and enjoyment with my partner		

Exercise 7A (cont.)

Common Problems That My Partner and I May Have	IBs I May Create About This Problem	RBs That I Can Use to Alleviate This This Problem
Other common problems my partner and I may have (specify)		

Exercise 7B: How Can My Partner and I Be Rational About Spending Money?

Question 1: What can my partner and I do if we spend foolishly and then beat ourselves mercilessly for being such awful fools?
Answer: _____
_____
_____
_____
_____
_____
_____
_____
_____
_____
_____
_____
_____
_____

Turn the page for REBT answers

1. We can rate our behavior, our foolish spending, as bad, foolish, ridiculous, or self-defeating. But we do not have to rate our *selves*, our *beings*, our *totality* in terms of this behavior; in fact, we do not have to rate our *selves* at all, even though we engage in the behavior and are responsible for engaging in it.

2. We can always choose to accept ourselves as good or okay persons, just because we are alive. When we choose to see ourselves as bad, rotten, or inadequate persons, we really *choose* to do so, and we can always choose *not* to do this, and to say to ourselves, "I am human. I am alive. As long as I am alive and human, I can see myself as a good person. Period."

3. Yes, we are persons who are doing this foolish thing, spending too much money. But we do many other good things (such as being kind to others) and many neutral things (such a watching TV). So we are only persons *who* spend too much money, and never really *good persons* or *rotten persons!*

Question 2: Do my partner and I need people to look up to us for spending as much as they do or for being lavish spenders or great savers?

Answer: _____

_____

_____

_____

_____

_____

_____

_____

_____

_____

_____

_____

_____

_____

Turn the page for the REBT answers

REBT Answers to Question 2:

1. No, we don't *need* people to look up to us for *anything*—for spending as much as they do, for being lavish spenders, or for being great savers. We *want* people to like us and look up to us, but we never *need* them to do so. If they don't and even if we do the wrong thing in their and our own eyes, we can always decide that what we did is wrong and stupid but that we, the doers of this deed, are *not* wrong, rotten, or stupid *persons*.

2. Because it is preferable for people to like us, and because they give us goodies and favors when they do, we may well decide to do our spending according to their wishes. But we don't *have* to agree with them and go along with them and can be happy even if they do not like what we do.

3. If people hate *us*, instead of only disliking our *behavior*, when we overspend or underspend, they are overgeneralizing about us and have a problem themselves. Too bad, if they have such a problem, but we can live with their disapproval.

Question 3: Are my partner and I real failures for not earning more money or for failing to save more money?

Answer: _____

_____

_____

_____

_____

_____

_____

_____

_____

_____

_____

_____

_____

_____

_____

_____

Turn the page for the REBT answers

REBT Answers to Question 3:

1. No. If we don't have more money than we now have, we are failing to make and keep as much as we would like to make and keep, but we are merely failing in this respect, and are succeeding in many other aspects of our life. A "failure" would always fail—and that is not us.

2. Failing to earn and save more money than we now do is highly inconvenient, if we really want more money, but that is *all* it is. It doesn't make *us*, as *people*, bad—unless we foolishly *think* that it does.

3. Earning and having more money than we now have may be very important to us. But it is not *all*-important, not *necessary*, not *sacred*.

4. Even if my partner and I failed at everything we did in life—which is most improbable—we would not be "real failures" in the sense of being damnable and undeserving of any good things in life. We would merely be persons with real handicaps and would still deserve to live and be helped by others who fail less.

Question 4: When my partner and I spend too much money, are we doing so because we really feel very anxious, depressed, or self-hating, and, rather than face these feelings, are we trying to distract ourselves by spending, by getting immediate satisfactions by doing so, and by temporarily feeling much better than we really feel underneath?

Answer: _____

_____

_____

_____

_____

_____

_____

_____

_____

_____

_____

_____

_____

_____

Turn the page for the REBT answers

REBT Answers to Question 4:

1. It is possible that we are spending to distract ourselves from our feelings of anxiety, depression, or self-hatred. Let us look at how we feel just before we do too much spending, and how we feel immediately afterward.

2. If we really are spending money to cover up our own negative feelings, we will thereby make ourselves *feel* better temporarily but not *get* better. In fact, by denying that we have these negative feelings, we will take away our chances of dealing with them and eliminating them.

3. When we deny our feelings of anxiety and depression, we are really telling ourselves: "It would be shameful to have such feelings! We would be no-goodniks for having them!" We therefore create symptoms *about* our symptoms—making ourselves depressed about our depression, or panicked about our anxiety. It is not *shameful*, but only *self-defeating*, to have neurotic symptoms. So we'd better acknowledge them fully—and then use REBT to reduce them instead of covering them up or temporarily distracting ourselves from them.

Exercise 7C: Do My Partner and I Spend too Much Money— and How Can We Stop?

Question 1: Does my partner's and my overspending prove that we are weak or stupid persons? If not, why not?

Answer: _____

_____

_____

_____

_____

_____

_____

_____

_____

_____

_____

_____

_____

Turn the page for the REBT answers

REBT Answers to Question 1:

1. No. It only proves, at worst, that we are behaving weakly and stupidly in this aspect of our lives.

2. In other respects, we may be acting quite strongly and intelligently.

3. Even if we always acted weakly and stupidly—which is most unlikely—we would be behaving foolishly but we still wouldn't be worthless, rotten persons, but people who had great handicaps. We would still deserve to live and enjoy ourselves simply because we are human and choose to live and enjoy life.

Question 2: Did our early upbringing make me or my partner an overspender? If not, why not?

Answer: _____

_____

_____

_____

_____

_____

_____

_____

_____

_____

_____

_____

_____

_____

_____

_____

_____

_____

_____

_____

Turn the page for the REBT answers

REBT Answers to Question 2:

No, our early upbringing probably did not make me or my partner an overspender because:

1. Even if our parents were overspenders and encouraged us to follow in their footsteps, we did not *have to* agree with and go along with them.

2. When we were children, we doubtless saw other people who were frugal and even penny-pinching. Why did we not follow *them?*

3. If our parents were thieves or murderers, would we have to imitate their kind of behavior? Of course not!

4. If our parents overspent, we could have noticed the hassles and disadvantages of their ways and could have chosen to avoid those hassles by behaving otherwise.

5. If we followed our parents' model and overspent because they did, we could have seen later how our overspending got us into trouble and therefore stopped it.

6. If we took our parents' preferences for overspending and made them into our own, we did not have to turn these preferences into absolutist musts, and we did not have to make ourselves compulsive overspenders.

7. No matter what goals and standards we adopted from our parents in our early lives, we have the ability to choose to adopt different ones today. So, as far as overspending is concerned, we'd better construct our *own* present standards and behaviors!

Question 3: What is low frustration tolerance (LFT)? How can I change it if I suffer from it?

Answer: _____

_____

_____

_____

_____

_____

_____

_____

_____

_____

_____

_____

_____

_____

_____

_____

_____

_____

_____

_____

_____

_____

_____

Turn the page for the REBT answers

REBT Answers to Question 3:

Low frustration tolerance means looking for immediate gratification even when it later brings me poor results (for example, smokers risk getting emphysema and lung cancer); refusing to do onerous tasks even when they would bring good results (for example, refusing to diet and exercise to lower my weight and thereby lower my blood pressure); defining a task or project as *too* hard to do and demanding that it *must* not be as hard as it is; choosing to believe that I can get good results by procrastinating on or avoiding a task when I most probably will get bad results (for example, telling myself that I need more time to get better data for a paper I am writing, when delaying writing it will most likely lead to my writing it frantically and badly at the last moment).

I can overcome low frustration tolerance (LFT) in several ways:

1. I can strongly convince myself that I don't *need* immediate gratification that would result in my later harm, even though I would definitely *like* to have it.

2. I can strongly convince myself that doing onerous tasks is hard but not *too* hard, that it is best to get them out of the way quickly, and that doing them (for example, exercising) won't kill me but not doing them well may!

3. I can show myself that no matter how hard certain tasks (like finishing a paper) are, it will be much *harder* if I don't do them.

4. I can write down a list of the disadvantages of procrastinating on or avoiding certain important tasks and read and think about these disadvantages several times every day to sink into my head the rational idea that I am *not* going to gain by delay and avoidance.

5. I can reinforce myself with something I find quite rewarding— such as music, reading, or socializing—every time I make myself do burdensome things that later lead to good results and every time I avoid immediate gratification that later leads to bad results.

6. I can penalize myself in some meaningful way—by doing something I really think is unpleasant—each time I indulge in harmful immediate gratification and each time I avoid doing burdensome things that will later lead to good results.

Question 4: Why is it better for my partner and I to have some long-range monetary goals and plans than to only stay with short-term objectives?

Answer: _____

_____

_____

_____

_____

_____

_____

_____

_____

_____

_____

_____

_____

_____

_____

_____

Turn the page for the REBT answers

REBT Answers to Question 4:

1. My short-range plans will soon be fulfilled or found wanting, and I will then have to take time and effort to revise them.

2. My short-term monetary goals—for example, renting a larger apartment—may sabotage my long-range and more important goals— such as saving money to buy a home.

3. Long-range goals give me a vital interest that may enjoyably last for a long period of time and help me nicely structure a large part of my life.

4. My long-range monetary goals are more likely to be achieved because I have a longer period of time to plan for and possibly revise them.

5. My long-range monetary goals will very likely help me provide substantially for my later years, while more short-range goals may by no means do this.

Question 5: If I am phobic about financial planning and stubbornly refuse to do it, what irrational beliefs am I probably telling myself?

Answer: _____

_____

_____

_____

_____

_____

_____

_____

_____

_____

_____

_____

_____

_____

_____

_____

_____

Turn the page for the REBT answers

REBT Answers to Question 5:

---

1. "I am unable to plan. An incompetent person like me would surely screw up my planning!"

2. "Suppose my financial plans don't work out. What a hopeless fool I would be!"

3. "My relatives and friends insist that I do financial planning when I really don't want to do it. To hell with them!"

4. "It takes too much time and effort to plan. It's not worth it!"

5. "No matter how well I plan, the country's whole financial system will doubtless be screwed up and I could easily have my plans go wrong. So what's the use of planning?"

Question 6: What can I tell myself about TV, magazine, radio, and other advertising that may influence me to not overspend?

Answer: _____

_____

_____

_____

_____

_____

_____

_____

_____

_____

_____

_____

_____

_____

_____

_____

_____

Turn the page for the REBT answers

REBT Answers to Question 6:

1. "The advertiser is distinctly interested in making money, not in my welfare!"

2. "No matter how good this merchandise is made to look, I don't *need* it!"

3. "I can think for myself and don't have to be so damned suggestible!"

4. "Even if the advertised product is desirable, it is hardly worth the money I will have to pay for it. Spending money on this product will deprive me of savings or of some other item that would be more useful."

Question 7: What can I say to my partner or my friends if they urge me to spend more money than is good for me to spend?
Answer: _____

_____

_____

_____

_____

_____

_____

_____

_____

_____

_____

_____

_____

_____

_____

Turn the page for the REBT answers

REBT Answers to Question 7:

1. "I'd be glad to go along with you, but frankly I can't afford it."

2. "I can see why you want to spend money on this thing, but it is just not the kind of thing that I want."

3. "You may think I'm cheap for not spending this amount of money, but I'd rather be thought cheap than do what I really don't want to do."

4. "I could probably afford to go along with the expenditure that you are suggesting, but it's just not what I'd like to spend my money on."

8

Getting Along Together and With Others

Up to now we have concentrated on how intimate partners can relate more effectively and enjoyably to each other. Most couples, however, do not live in isolation, and how they relate to friends, relatives, neighbors, and others can importantly affect them as individuals and as a couple. Using similar REBT principles to those we have described for improved couplehood, you can also relate better to other people.

Before we explore other-relating, let's ask ourselves whether getting along with other people is a reasonable goal. Wouldn't it be better if we all decided we wanted to learn to be wonderful people and become leaders in the community and be admired and respected for the leadership we have provided? Not exactly. While these and various other goals may be desirable for some of us, it is usually better for us first to learn how to get along with people. After you are getting along, if you have the interest, skills, time, and energy to become a community leader, splendid.

Even the goal of associating with others often cannot be approached as directly as you might want. The main reason for this is simple: as we have seen in our discussion of couples, Person A—you, let's say—cannot change anyone's behavior other than your own. No, not even the behavior of your partner, Person B. So where will you get if you tell Persons C and D, your arrogant and grouchy neighbors, to behave differently in order to enable you to enjoy them more? Nowhere! In addition, if you focus on how to alter your own behavior in order (hopefully) to change Persons C through Z, you can find this a very time-and-energy consuming enterprise—with no guarantee of success!

What can you do to enhance your relations with others? First, determine how you can *enjoy* being with others *even* when they behave badly. You can, of course, try to change other people (lots of luck!). And you can try to change yourself when you are with them so that you help them act less and less obnoxiously than they usually do. But rather than count on changed behavior from them, try to enjoy yourself more *without* such changes.

Second, agree with your partner that you will both check on each other's efforts to enjoy yourselves more with others (as well as with one another). This cross-check helps you see how "right" you are in viewing others and may increase your enjoy of them.

The work of relating better to others mainly consists of your striving to overcome your own major irrational ideas. As a human, you may have inherited tendencies to think unhealthily or you may have had them laid heavily upon you in your early years. Also, some of your irrationality may stem from your recent thoughts about unfortunate experiences that led you to create and cling dearly to destructive thoughts, feelings, and actions. However you "got that way," only you can make yourself function more realistically and enjoyably today.

Your main laboratory for experimenting, testing, and reworking your IBs can be your relationships with others. You are also particularly fortunate, as we said above, if you have the advantage and the fun of a living-as-a-couple laboratory.

MRB stands for "more rational beliefs." We are not trying to do your thinking for you (it wouldn't be of any use to you even if we tried), but we are giving you some less irrational and more realistic thought patterns to kick around in your own head and to discuss with your partner. Maybe some of the more rational beliefs we present (reshaped to your own personality and your own couplehood) will be helpful. Maybe you and your partner will throw them all out and come up with *MRB*s that have strictly your own seals on them.

CHANGING YOUR IRRATIONAL BELIEFS
ABOUT OTHERS

Following are some important IBs about others that you can explore and work at changing.

IB: "I must be totally approved as a person regardless of how I behave."

MRB: "I will strive to do what I consider enjoyable and desirable. That usually includes accepting some of the people who show that they like or accept me as a person. But since people in their reactions tend to jump from rating my particular behavior to rating me as a total person, they are overgeneralizing and will not accurately rate me globally. Even if I could somehow get people to react to the "real me" (which is an inaccurate abstraction), what are my chances of having them react to this "real me" as totally lovable? Very slim! I may learn something helpful from other people's views of me, but what I learn should be balanced by what I learn from other sources."

IB: "To be worthwhile as a person I must prove to others that I am outstanding in whatever I do. To fail to do so shows that I am a failure or an inadequate person who doesn't deserve people's approval."

MRB: "It is nice if I perform well and am therefore approved by others—nice but not necessary. And my performance has nothing to do with my worth as a person."

IB: "I should judge people by who they seem to be—as *good* or *bad* individuals. If I judge them to be wrong, bad, or evil, they deserve to be damned and punished."

MRB: "Because all people are human and hence fallible, I and others will surely misbehave part of the time. None of us *is* good or bad, though we all *do* "good" and "bad" things. I can give people unconditional other-acceptance (UOA) and only rate their *deeds* and not their *selves*. I will try to help them act better but refuse to damn *them* when they don't."

IB: "Since REBT says I am not to worry about what other people think and what they tell me I ought to do, I'll always do whatever I feel like doing whenever I feel like doing it. Today I feel like staying home from work and lying on the beach smoking pot all day. So whatever else other people may be expecting, I'll avoid working. Fun's fun, man."

MRB: "Let me face it. Indulging in immediate gratification that later leads to grim results (such as getting lung cancer from smoking) is hardly *fun*. I can enjoy life more if I don't cop out but promptly and unrebelliously do difficult and unpleasant tasks for which I have responsibility. I can vigilantly try to distinguish between short-term and long-term hedonism. I won't always avoid immediate fun, but when it seriously distracts me from my commitments, I'd better be responsible to myself and to others and postpone the 'fun' till later. REBT never says I am not to be concerned *at all* about what other people think of me and my behavior, but only that I'd better not be *over*-concerned and worry *too much* about what they think."

IB: "My partner must take me the way I am. I have been molded into the kind of person that I am. The past cannot be altered, and I must go on deeply reacting in the same way that I always have."

MRB: "My past is not all-important. If I rethink my old assumptions and rework my past habits (and check from time to time with my partner on how much I am changing), I can minimize the undesirable influences from my childhood and adolescence. I can learn valuable lessons from studying my past, but I do not need to consider myself enslaved by it. Today is tomorrow's past: let's see what I can do to make it better. I hope that my partner accepts *me* with my *failings*. But to help myself and to improve our relationship, I'd better work on some of those failings!"

IB: "Since the REBT goal is to enjoy myself as much as I can, I will make as few commitments as possible and only arrange for free time, where nothing is expected of me and no responsibilities are laid on me. That's real happiness!"

MRB: "I have had my happiest times when I have been fully committed to and involved in action of some kind. I shall search and find and develop activities that challenge me and provide me with long-term expanding interest and development. I shall also try to help my partner, individually and as a couple, be committed and responsible, and thereby improve our relationship and our lives."

GETTING ALONG WITH OTHER PEOPLE AS A COUPLE

As we have noted in this chapter, getting along with other people— and especially with your partner—leads to decreased disturbance and increased happiness within and outside of your couplehood. This includes, in many cases, you and your partner getting along with other people—especially with your family members, close friends, and business associates—*together.*

You may avoid this problem, of course, by rarely having close contact with your partner's family, friends, or job associates. But is this practical—or desirable? Usually, you and s/he will want some of these contacts. Either of you may want the other to be reasonably friendly with, say, your relatives, long-standing friends, and close associates. You both may "intellectually" agree that this would be desirable, but actually find each other's intimates too boring, stupid, hostile, clinging, or otherwise obnoxious. You may then—either of you—avoid, hate, fight with, or severely criticize them. If you do, you and your partner may well have a problem!

Liane, for example, was usually friendly and warm to her husband's relatives and friends but loathed Jake's mother, Doris, whom she (and several other people) considered to be supercritical, mean, and utterly dependent upon Jake. While he acknowledged his mother's "faults," he loved her deeply, pitied her, and took good care of her, especially after his father died. Liane, using a million excuses, rarely saw Doris and when she was practically forced to do so, seethed with resentment and was often rude to her. Jake tried to help Liane to at least tolerate Doris better, but failed to do so, and was torn between his allegiance to his wife and his mother. He practically forced Liane to see me (Dr. Ellis) for therapy.

As is common in cases like Liane's, I acknowledged her rational preferences about Doris—to avoid her as much as possible and encourage Jake to be less devoted to her. But we, Liane and I, soon uncovered several IBs she strongly held to make herself angry, depressed, and self-hating: (1) "Doris *must not* be as disturbed and rotten as she is!", (2) "I *can't stand* being with her or talking to her on the phone for even a few minutes!", (3) "Jake should completely see through her and stop idiotically taking care of her!", (4) "I am angry at Jake and am destroying my relationship with him—as I absolutely must not do!", (5) "our two children must see how loathsome their grandmother, Doris, is and not love her the way they do!"

I found that helping Liane give up these IBs was quite a task, and for several weeks I thought I would never reach her. She found Doris so nauseatingly "hypocritical"—deliberately warm, loving, and forgiving to Jake and her grandchildren, and mean and nasty to Liane and just about everyone else. So she concluded that Doris was *able* to control her feelings and behaviors and act consistently polite, but she deliberately *refused* to do so. Liane was incensed at this "hypocrisy."

I got at least a foot in the door in disputing Liane's IBs when I showed her that she, too, was "hypocritically" *able* to act well to many people but presumably *not able* to change or suppress her hostility to Doris. Moreover, she, Liane, "hypocritically" let herself love and hate her own husband, Jake.

My showing Liane her own "hypocritical" inconsistencies, and her own *ability* to control her hatred when she really tried to do so, finally got to her and she began to give up her deep resentment by changing her irrational *demands* for Doris's and Jake's acting well to strong *preferences*. She convinced herself, "I really *wish* Doris were less mean and overly critical of me, *but* she doesn't *have* to be. Let her remain—as she will—as sick as she is in these respects."

As she changed some of her own incensing beliefs, I showed

Liane how to plan and scheme, and then how to act, *together* with Jake, when Doris visited them. Liane, for example, would work on her own incipient hostility and deliberately *seem* to agree with Doris about her being overly nice to their children; and Jake would firmly refuse some of Doris's inconsiderate demands on him, while working on his own guilt about not giving in to her. Liane and Jake *acted* so well with Doris on many planned-in-advance occasions that Liane often *felt* more forgiving and less hostile to her mother-in-law and Jake *felt* less guilty and firmer in resisting his mother's inconsiderate demands.

This case shows the general REBT procedure to help you and your partner relate better to yourself, each other, and your and his/her close associates. First, look for, find, and actively dispute your IBs that are interfering with this relating. Second, replace these IBs with RBs and preferences. Third, discuss with your partner your own and his or her dysfunctional demands that are interfering with your relationships with her/him and your close associates. Fourth, plan to act harmoniously and enjoyably when s/he is together with you and your intimates and you are together with his/her intimates.

When you actually meet together with each other's close associates, here are some questions to consider and helpful rules to know:

1. How close are your and his/her relations with other people? Casual, moderately close, really intimate?

2. How do you want your partner to feel and behave about your intimates—whether that means really feel or pretend to feel?

3. How does your partner want you to feel and behave about your intimates—again, whether that means really feel or pretend to feel?

4. Can you and your partner be comfortable with seeing your and his/her intimates always together, sometimes together, occasionally together, never together? Just because you or s/he is close to family members or other people does *not* mean that you always *have to* see them as a couple.

5. In ticklish cases—where, for example, you and your partner would prefer to see an ex-lover or someone either of you detest alone—fully agree upon the rules of how often, how long, where

and when, and other conditions of meeting this person or these people.

6. When you meet each other's intimates together, plan how you and your partner will usually act with them. Where and when? What will you usually do together? What will you particularly avoid saying and doing? Discuss this with each other before the meeting.

7. Try to figure out how you and your partner's relatives and friends can actually help or enhance your relationship. What role can they play in aiding it and helping the two of you get closer?

8. Experiment with your mutually arrived-at goals in these respects. See if they work—and change them if they don't!

9. If feelings or relationships with you and your partner's intimates seem to be becoming an obstacle to your own relationship, honestly discuss it, however difficult. See what you can do to remove these "obstacles."

10. Agree on suitable ways to handle your and your partner's relations with intimates, try them out for awhile, and from time to time review them to see if they are still working satisfactorily. If not, back to the drawing board!

Are the IBs we have just looked at, as well as your self-defeating actions, the only ways you can mess up yourself, your relationship with your partner, and both of your relationships with others? By no means! Because of your human limitations, you, like all people, may well have a boundless capacity for thinking up ways of defeating, downing, and even destroying yourself and your relationships. So watch it!

Are your more rational, healthy beliefs guaranteed to put your irrational ones permanently to rest? We hope you have not only read but *practiced* enough REBT by now to know better than that. Face it: Vigilance and hard work will keep you functioning more healthily and more enjoyably—but not perfectly.

Nor will you, by reading and heeding this chapter, get along perfectly well with your partner and with other people. We hope you will and are pretty sure that you can, but we give you no guarantees—only a fairly high degree of probability.

EXERCISES FOR CHAPTER 8

This chapter emphasized minimizing your self-defeating IBs and changing them into self-helping MRBs. And while this seems clear and obvious, it isn't as easy to do as it often seems. Many of our clients for over four decades now have promptly grasped and agreed with the "truth" of seeing their IBs and substituting RBs for them. Easily and quickly grasped. Easily and quickly agreed. But not easily achieved!

Some, of course, haven't really tried to change their IBs. "Oh, yes, you're right. My belief that I absolutely *need* other people's approval is largely false—and will get me nowhere, with them and with myself." "Right! My partner can't really love me completely at all times. No one can! I'd better give up believing that nonsense— or else I'll continually be anxious and angry. What rot!"

Good agreement—but still little change. You beautifully tell yourself sensible dating, relating, and mating philosophies. Still no real conviction about them. Only some mighty sensible beliefs—at most!

Suppose, then, that you agree with the MRBs described in this chapter. How do you *really* convince yourself of them? How do you get yourself to largely *follow* them?

In 1962, a social psychologist, Robert Abelson, pointed out that people have both *cool* and *hot* cognitions. I (Dr. Ellis) quickly saw that he was on the right track, and added that people also have warm, as well as cool and hot beliefs. Let us explain.

Cool beliefs are your descriptions of people and things, without positive or negative evaluations of them. For example, "This is a table. I see that it is round" or "Peter or Patricia asked me for a date. He or she seems to favor me."

Warm beliefs are your evaluations of your observations and descriptions, such as "I don't like this round table. I wish it were square" and "I like Peter or Patricia's asking me for a date. Good!"

Hot beliefs give your very strong evaluation of your observations and descriptions. For example, "I really hate this round table. I'm going to do my best to get rid of it and get a square one instead" or "I am completely thrilled with Peter or Patricia's asking me for a date. This is the best thing that has happened to me all year!"

Hot insistent beliefs give you very strong and demanding evaluations of your observations and descriptions, like "This round table is really disgusting! It must not remain here! I *can't stand* it. I am going to get an axe and chop it up" or "Peter or Patricia's asking me for a date is so desirable that s/he must go through with it and do whatever I want on the date! I *must not* be deprived in any way by him/her. It would be *awful* if I were. I couldn't bear it!"

Following Abelson, REBT assumes that when you are encouraged by your IBs to create unhealthy feelings and behaviors, and that when you do so consistently and have trouble changing your beliefs to preferences, thus creating healthier feelings and behaviors, you tend to hold on to your IBs very hotly—to forcefully, vigorously, and powerfully (consciously and/or unconsciously) cling to them. Therefore, if you merely dispute them mildly and moderately you may keep them *along with* the RBs or effective new philosophies that you *say* that you now believe.

When you dispute your IBs and come up with rational coping self-statements with which to replace them, you can easily "see" that these RBs are "true" or "helpful," but you may only lightly and ineffectually believe them. Thus, you can "intellectually" see that smoking is harmful, but "emotionally" believe, "It really won't harm *me*" or "I can get away with it," or "No matter how hard I try, I *can't* stop smoking!" You then may well continue to smoke!

In exercises 8A and 8B, you will figure out some rational coping self-statements, perhaps writing them out on a 3 × 5 index card to show yourself the various *reasons* why they make sense and will help you. Say them to yourself five or ten times a day and repeat them forcefully and vigorously each time until you feel that you *really* understand them and convincingly believe them. Strongly say them to yourself while you solidly *think about* why they are accurate and helpful. You will than tend to achieve "emotional" as well as "intellectual" insight into your RBs.

Sample Exercise 8A: Using Forceful and Persistent Rational Coping Self-Statements

Rational Coping Self-Statements About Getting Along With My Partner That I Can Forcefully and Convincingly Tell Myself Until I Solidly Believe and Act on Them

I would really like to find a suitable partner, but I definitely *don't have to* find one. I won't be *as* happy by myself but I can always find *a great deal of happiness* if I remain unmated. If I am unmated, I will *try like hell* to enjoy myself and lead a full life.

I *fully realize* that it is difficult for me to find a permanent suitable partner. Very difficult—but *not impossible!* There are literally thousands—or millions!—of good partners in the world for me. And I can—if I *keep looking and experimenting*—find one. I *can*, I *can!* So I will unfrantically *keep looking, looking, looking!*

Yes, my partner *may well* be unfair to me and often. S/he *may* criticize me unduly, lie to me about something, or spend too much of our money on foolish things and unjustly deprive me. *Too bad!* My partner will *often* be far from fair! That is human nature! *Tough!* But s/he has many good points, too. *Many!* I *can* enjoy him or her *in spite of* some unfairness. It won't kill me! I can *accept* him or her with her/his faults. Because *it's worth it—really worth it!*

I *can* stand important disagreements with my partner. I may never like their position, never agree, but I can *agree to disagree!* I never have to get her/him to agree with me—though that would be great! Disagreements are interesting. I can learn from them. So can s/he. We can enjoy our disagreements. And *really* enjoy being honest about them and letting each other have them—that can be *fantastic!*

Yes, I really *dislike* doing annoying or boring things with my partner. But *I'd better* sometimes do them, without carping and screaming. Without nastily rebelling. Some of them *go with* a

Exercise 8A (cont.)

good relationship. My partner may enjoy them and I can enjoy his/her enjoyment! Sure I can get away with balking and goofing. But is it *worth* it? Rarely! So I often *will* do what I don't like to please my partner. To enhance our relationship. *I can! I will!*

Exercise 8A: Some Rational Coping Self-Statements About Getting Along With My Partner That I Can Forcefully Convince Myself of Until I Solidly Believe and Act on Them

_____

_____

_____

_____

_____

_____

_____

_____

_____

_____

_____

_____

_____

_____

_____

_____

_____

_____

_____

_____

_____

_____

_____

_____

Sample Exercise 8B: Using Forceful and Persistent Rational Coping Self-Statements About Getting Along With My Partner's Close Associates and Intimates That I Can Tell Myself Until I Solidly Believe and Act on Them

I don't have to *like* my partner's close associates and intimates. They have a perfect *right* to be as unlikeable as they *are*. I probably can't *stop* them from being obnoxious but I *can stand it*. I am *making myself* angry at them and damning *them* for their unfortunate *behavior*. I can darned well stop my damnation and then tolerate them much better.

My partner is free to like or dislike my close associates and intimates. S/he is wrong if s/he hates *them* and not merely their *behavior*, but s/he has a right to be wrong! I would distinctly *prefer* him/her to feel and act well when s/he meets them. But s/he doesn't *have to* do so!

I am foolishly harming myself and my relationship with my partner when I ignore or act badly toward his/her close associates and intimates. But I am *not* a fool for doing so—just a *person who* acts stupidly. Let me work on myself to feel and act less angrily, and do my best to *accept* his/her friends even if I never greatly like them. *I and we* will thereby benefit!

There is no *necessity* for my partner to act well with my close friends and associates, though that would be *preferable*. Even if s/he is prejudiced against them, I can accept and care for him/her because of his/her many other good traits. I can dislike several of the things s/he does, but if I dislike *him/her* for doing them I shall help ruin our relationship.

I *can* go to the trouble of finding out how my partner feels and acts about my close associates and intimates, and I will! It's *worth* discussing this with him/her and planning how we act when we are together with our intimates. If either or both of us has IBs that are encouraging us to feel and act badly in this respect, I *can* work with him/her to find and change them.

If I or my partner am over-involved with some of our close associates and intimates, which thereby interferes with our relation-

Exercise 8B (cont.)

ship, I can honestly discuss this with him/her and agree how, where, and under what conditions I and s/he will continue to have contact with these other people.

When my partner and I agree on how we will handle our relationships with close associates and intimates, so as to not seriously interfere with our closeness with each other, we shall review our feelings and actions in this respect from time to time and work to change our relationship-sabotaging behaviors.

*Exercise 8B: Forceful and Persistent Rational Coping Self-Statements
About Getting Along With My Partner's Close Associates and Intimates
That I Can Tell Myself Until I Solidly Believe and Act on Them*

_____

_____

_____

_____

_____

_____

_____

_____

_____

_____

_____

_____

_____

_____

_____

_____

_____

_____

_____

As Aesop demonstrated thousands of years ago in "The Fox and the Grapes," we are great rationalizers and excusers. We often try to fool others, but—more importantly—we try to fool ourselves, especially with our own rational coping self-statements. Even when you say them forcefully and persistently—as illustrated in exercise 8A— you can easily parrot them and, honestly and truly, have important hidden objections to and quibbles with them.

Windy Dryden, one of the most prolific and capable writers about REBT, has come up with a forceful method of overcoming this kind of insincere parroting—by showing you how to go out of your way and argue with your own rational coping self-statements until you answer your hidden objections to them and vigorously reaffirm them in a more self-convincing manner.

Sample Exercise 8C: Arguing With and Reaffirming Rational Coping Self-Statements

Rational Coping Self-Statements That I May Lightly Believe	My Arguing With My Own Rational Coping Self-Statement	My Firm Answers to My Arguing My Rational Coping Self-Statements That I Lightly Believe
Although I'd *like* to find a suitable partner, I don't *have to* find one and can be happy by myself.	Yes, I won't *die* from not finding a suitable partner but I'd be *much less* happy and therefore depressed.	(1) Do I *have to be* much less happy? I might even be happi*er!* I can avoid and miss out on the *hassles* and *restrictions* of being mated. (2) Even if I were *less* happy without a partner, I could still be reasonably happy. Even if I were *un*happy I would never have to make myself depressed *about* my unhappiness. I could merely be *sad* and *frustrated.*
Though it may be *quite difficult* for me to find a suitable partner, it is not *im*possible! If I keep looking and looking I can still find one.	Yes, but suppose I look and look and never *do* find one? That would really be *awful!*	(1) It is most unlikely that I'll *never* find one—especially if I don't demand that I find the *best* possible partner. (2) If—which is *very* unlikely—I never find one, I can, really *can* find distinct happiness, if I *think* I can and arrange to find it!

Exercise 8C (cont.)

Rational Coping Self-Statements That I May Lightly Believe	My Arguing With My Own Rational Coping Self-Statements	My Firm Answers to My Arguing With My Rational Coping Self-Statements That I Lightly Believe
Too bad if my partner is unfair! I can *still* enjoy many aspects of him/her. It's *worth* staying and continuing our relationship.	Yes, but if s/he is *really* unfair, that would make anyone, including me, angry. I *never* could stand that!	(1) His/her degree of unfairness would be very *displeasing*. But I still don't have to *demand* fairness and make *myself* angry. (2) I can always choose to *un*angrily leave my partner. (3) If I act lovingly in spite of the unfairness, I may induce him/her to be fair. (4) At the worst, I *could* stand the unfairness and still benefit from being with my partner. Although I naturally *dislike* important disagreements with my partner, I can agree to disagree. Disagreements can even be interesting.
Although I naturally *dislike* important disagreements with my partner, I can agree to disagree. Disagreements can be very interesting.	Yes, but we often disagree *so often* that that's really pretty awful! And our disagreements are so repetitive that they are damned boring. I *can't stand* them.	(1) No matter how often we disagree, it's only *awful* if I take our disagreements too seriously—which I never *have to* do! (2) Even though our disagreements are repetitive, if I really *accept*

Exercise 8C (cont.)

Rational Coping Self-Statements That I May Lightly Believe	My Arguing With My Own Rational Coping Self-Statement	My Firm Answers to My Arguing With My Rational Coping Self-Statements That I Lightly Believe
		them and *not* make an issue out of them we'll deal with them quickly and unboringly. If not, I *can* still stand them.
Although I dislike doing annoying or boring things with my partner, I still do them and can enhance our relationship.	Yes, but what kind of a relationship is this if s/he keeps making me do so many annoying and boring things. I might as well mate with a porcupine.	Just about *all* relationships include many annoying and boring things. Do I really want to be *alone?* Look how annoying and boring that would be!

Exercise 8C

Rational Coping Self-Statements That I May Lightly Believe	My Arguing With My Own Rational Coping Self-Statements	My Firm Answers To My Arguing With My Rational Coping Self-Statements That I Lightly Believe
_____	_____	_____
_____	_____	_____
_____	_____	_____
_____	_____	_____
_____	_____	_____
_____	_____	_____
_____	_____	_____
_____	_____	_____
_____	_____	_____
_____	_____	_____
_____	_____	_____
_____	_____	_____
_____	_____	_____
_____	_____	_____
_____	_____	_____
_____	_____	_____

Exercise 8D: Reverse Role-Playing About My Upsetness About My Partner's Relatives

To use this REBT emotive-evocative method, you pick one of your IBs that you strongly hold and resist changing. Get a friend to hold on to this IB very firmly and rigidly, while you—playing a sensible person—persist at trying to talk him or her out of it. One of your reverse role-playing dialogues might go like this.

Your Friend (holding your IBs): I just won't allow it. I won't allow my partner, May, to continue to see Jake. Not only is he a cretin but I'd be a weak slob to allow her to see him.

You: How does allowing May to see Jake make *you* a weak slob? Even if he is cretinish, how does her seeing him affect *you?*

Your Friend: Obviously he's still after her ass—and will try to get it. What kind of man am I if I allow this?

You: What the devil does this have to do with your manhood? Let's suppose he is trying to get May into bed with him. Can't she resist? Is *she* a weakling?

Your Friend: It's too risky! I'm taking a foolish chance. I'll never forgive myself if she succumbs. And everyone will see what a stupid weakling I am!

You: Let's suppose the worst: May does go to bed with Jake. So that's bad. You trusted her too far and you made a mistake. How does that make you a wholly stupid person? Even if people *think* you are, does that *make* you one?

Your Friend: But what a mistake! I should have known! People would be right about me!

You: Maybe about your foolish *acts.* But not about *you.* You *aren't* your actions.

Your Friend: You damned well are! Certainly in this case—let's face it!

You: Now *you're* overgeneralizing. *You* do millions of acts. Most of them, in fact, pretty good. So even if *this* one is foolish, how does that make *you* a total fool?

Your Friend: Lots of people will think I am!

Exercise 8D (cont.)

You: Let them! They're wrong! You won't like what they *think*. But if you're quite determined, you'll always accept *you*, no matter what you do.

    Your Friend: That's really great. If I do that I'll be able to give up my nutty jealousy. No matter what my partner does, I'll still be able to accept *me*. Her actions don't *make* me anything, no more than yours do.
    You: I think you're right about that. Yes—work on that.

Whatever emotional problem you have with your mate, about upsetting yourself about his or her relations with friends or relatives, or about anything else, you can have a friend play your upset role, stick rigidly to it, and let you talk yourself (played by them) out of your disturbance. Try it and see!

9

How to Be Happy in Spite of Your Blasted In-Laws

As we have already noted, this book is not merely an updated version of our 1961 manual, *A Guide to a Successful Marriage*. This book focuses on partnerships and relationships that go beyond conventional mating and includes new REBT ideas and practices developed since the 1960s.

However, to show you how some of the principles of REBT have consistently been useful to many individuals and couples since we started to practice them, we have taken one of the chapters from our earlier book and have included it here with a few minor revisions.

It may seem a shame to spoil a fine, forward-looking book on relationships such as this one with the unsavory topic of in-law relations, but a relationship will hardly be fine or forward-looking if this topic is neglected. Of the many couples whom we see every year for marriage counseling, it is surprising what a high percentage are in more or less difficulty partly or mainly because of serious in-law problems.

Nor, in almost all instances, is there any good reason for this. Not that in-laws cannot be highly difficult, dunce-like, and even dangerous persons. They can be. Nor that wives and husbands cannot be childishly and exasperatingly bound to their parents. They can be. Nonetheless, according to the basic principles of REBT, much intense and prolonged unhappiness that is not specifically caused by physical pain or deprivation is illegitimate and unethical. And that goes for misery about in-laws.

Take, by the way of illustration, the case of the Ms. When Mr. and Mrs. M first came to see me (Dr. Ellis), both insisted that they had just about the worst in-law problem in the world and they were seriously considering getting divorced in order to solve the problem. Mr. M alleged that his wife was completely devoted to her mother and that the mother hated him bitterly and did everything possible to break up their marriage. His mother-in-law feigned all kinds of illnesses, he said, in order to keep her daughter continually attached to her, and, far from ever trying to get along with Mr. M, the mother-in-law frankly said that his presence made her sick and that she never wanted to see him, if possible. Also, he claimed, she tried to alienate his thirteen-year-old daughter from him by telling the child what a terrible person he was.

When I heard her side of the story, Mrs. M did not claim that her husband was overly attached to his parents; in fact, she said that he really didn't seem to care for them at all. But, because he had been roundly indoctrinated by them with a sense of family obligation, he insisted on visiting his parents (who lived quite a distance away) at least once a week. In addition he never wanted to miss a single affair in which his very large family was involved. Again, complained Mrs. M, it would have been different if he really liked his family members and wanted to be with them on birthdays, anniversaries, and other occasions, but he just went, she contended, because he felt obligated. Such craven obedience to family protocol, said Mrs. M, was positively disgusting, and she didn't see why she had to suffer by being dragged along to so many of her husband's family gatherings just because he was such a moral coward.

I started work with Mr. M. During the first few weeks I saw him, his wife was busy taking care of her mother, who had just had her third so-called heart attack (entirely invented, insisted Mr. M) that year. She had no time to come to joint therapy sessions with him and me. As is usual in these cases, I began by assuming that his story about his wife and her mother was absolute gospel, and that he was not significantly exaggerating the facts involved. I was quite sure that Mrs. M, when I saw her, would tell a quite different story; but I deliberately assumed that the husband's story of his in-law difficulties was correct.

"Let us suppose," I said to Mr. M, "that you are describing the situation with your mother-in-law quite accurately, and that she actually is the kind of a woman you say she is. Why are you so upset about the situation?"

"What do you mean, why am I upset!" he fairly screamed at me. "Wouldn't you be, wouldn't anyone be upset if this sort of thing were going on in his home, and going on for the last fifteen years, mind you! Isn't that a good reason for me to be upset?"

"No," I calmly replied, looking him squarely in the eyes. "It isn't."

"It isn't! Then what is, then? What *is* a good reason to get upset?"

"Nothing," I just as calmly replied. "I never heard a good reason for anyone seriously upsetting themselves about anything."

"Oh, piddle! You don't really mean that. You're just saying that to—well, I don't know why you're saying it, but you just are."

"No, I'm deadly serious. I never heard of a good reason for anyone making themselves upset about anything. Even about physical pain. I see no reason to depress yourself. If you have a toothache, I certainly don't expect you to like it or be deliriously happy about it. But enraging yourself will hardly cure it or make it better. What's the point, then, of driving yourself into despair?"

"But how can—how can I help it, damn it? How can I help getting upset?"

"Very simply: Stop telling yourself the drivel you are telling yourself to make yourself miserable."

"Drivel? What drivel?"

"You know. Drivel such as: 'Oh, my God, how can she do this to me?' And: 'That lousy bitchy mother-in-law of mine, I hope she drops dead!' and: 'I just *can't stand* going on like this, with my wife acting in that perfectly idiotic and vicious manner!' And so on, and so forth."

"I can't see anything drivel-ish about that," sulked Mr. M. "She *is* a lousy bitch, my mother-in-law, and I hope she *does* drop dead. No, I can't see anything drivel-ish at all in that."

"Obviously, you can't, or you wouldn't keep repeating that nonsense to yourself. But when I convince you, as I intend to do, that it is utter bosh, real blather, to keep infecting yourself with this misery-creating stuff, you will probably stop doing so. And, lo and behold! Your horror will vanish."

"Quite a trick—if you can do it!"

"Yes. But it's trickier than you think. For actually, I intend to persuade *you* to do it—to get *you* to change your thinking and stop telling yourself that drivel. For I can't, of course, do it for you. I can convince you, perhaps, that what you're telling yourself is nonsense. But unless, finally, I get *you* to desist from feeding yourself this pap and get you, instead, to tell yourself good sense, all my sessions with you will go to waste."

"I still say: quite a trick—if you can do it!"

"Quite. But let's get back to the problem. You're off the wall, I insist, not because of the way your mother-in-law is—and I am taking your word, mind you, that she is that way—but because of the nonsense you're telling yourself *about* the way she is. Instead of forcefully telling yourself the truth, namely: 'That's the way the old gal is. Too bad, but there's nothing I can do to change her at her age, so I'd just better accept the way she is and stop incensing myself about it,' you're quite falsely telling yourself: 'How can she be the way she is? She *ought* not be the way she is! She *absolutely must not* be the unfair way she indubitably is!' and similar drivel."

"I still can't see why it's drivel."

"It's really very simple, if you look at it (which you're not really doing). To ask how a woman can be the way she is when, quite patently, she *is* that way is the worst nonsense under the sun. And to say that an old woman like your mother-in-law, who has been born and raised to be the way she is, *ought* not be that way is equivalent to saying that it *ought* not rain when it is raining. Also, to say that she must not be unfair when she *is* unfair is like saying the sky must not be blue because you'd *prefer* it to be some other color. It is *unfortunate* that your mother-in-law is not acting the way you'd *like* her to act. But you don't have to create a *horror* out of this *misfortune*."

"So you think that I should just accept my mother-in-law the way she is, whatever harm she inflicts on my wife, my child, and myself, and just let it go at that?"

"No, I don't think anything of the sort. I think that you should *first* accept her the way she is—by which I mean stop senselessly damning the poor woman for being as disturbed as she is. And, then, after you manage to accept her in the sense of not damning her, you can, of course, try to change her—or, more practically, perhaps change you're wife's attitude toward your mother-in-law, so that it doesn't matter too much how your mother-in-law behaves.

"The way you're doing things now—making yourself terribly upset about your mother-in-law and the way she unfortunately is—you haven't any chance of changing her (except for the worse). What is perhaps more important, you are ceaselessly antagonizing your own wife, and haven't any chance of changing her attitude toward her mother, either—except, again, for the worse. Now how is all *that* kind of behavior doing you any good?"

"Doesn't look like it is doing me much good at all, does it?" Mr. M rather sheepishly admitted.

"No, it certainly doesn't. So I don't care if you ever get to love the old gal, or care for her at all. But just as long as you waste your time and energy, as you have been doing for fifteen years, hating her, you're almost bound to make matters much worse. Moreover and perhaps more important, you're also bound to keep yourself decidedly upset. And what's the percentage in that?"

"Very little, I have to say."

"Darn right, very little. So I still point out: It's not, no, it's positively not, what your mother-in-law or your wife is doing that's upsetting you; it's only your silly childish, unrealistic *attitude* toward what they're doing that is making you miserable. And if you can take an honest and full look at your own attitude and then question and challenge it and give it a good kick in the teeth—which you definitely can, since *you* are the one who originally adopted it and have ever since been maintaining it—then practically nothing that your mother-in-law and your wife can or will do will seriously upset you. You won't *like*, naturally, many of the things they do; but you definitely will not seriously upset yourself, needlessly and gratuitously, by telling yourself—falsely, falsely, I still say—that what you don't like is *terrible, horrible*, and *awful*."

Naturally I didn't quite convince Mr. M, in the course of this session, that all his hostility and gut-gnashing about his mother-in-law and wife were pointless, that he was mainly upsetting himself in this connection, and that he could and preferably should stop doing so. But after several more sessions of the same kind of forceful teaching of REBT, reason and I began to win out, and one day Mr. M came in and said:

"You know, these sessions seem to be doing me some good. The other day—I would hardly have believed it a few weeks ago—my mother-in-law pulled one of her very worst tantrums. She not only got my wife to run to her side again, as usual, but started her rumpus at four in the morning, when we were soundly sleeping. She said she was having another of those so-called heart attacks again. Of course, as usual, my wife fell for the whole thing, and insisted on running off to see her and getting me up, no less, to drive her there, even though she knew I had a cold myself and hardly felt like going out at that time, in the middle of the night. Ordinarily, I would have been fit to be tied, and probably would have had a battle royal with her, and ended up seething about it for days.

"But, almost to my own surprise, I said—this time, I said to myself, that is, and *not* to my wife—'Well, there it goes again. Just as I knew it would, and was predicting to myself last night. The old bat's at it, as usual, and of course my wife, poor misguided soul that she is, can't resist her yet. Well, no help for it right now. Too bad, but no help for it. Since I have to go anyway, I might as well do with as much good grace as possible, as Dr. Ellis would say, and at least not give *myself* a hard time in the process.'

"And, believe it or not, I *didn't* give myself a hard time. Though I certainly didn't *enjoy* driving Martha to see her mother, I wasn't particularly unhappy about it either. And the old bat, when she saw what kind of a calm mood I was in, even seemed to take things better for a change and wasn't so negative against me. You know, you're quite right: it *can* be done. You can think yourself out of anger just as, as you keep telling me, you think yourself into it. The other night was quite an eye-opener for me!"

And thereafter for the next few weeks of psychotherapy, Mr. M continued to work on himself and to improve significantly in his attitudes toward his wife and his mother-in-law. So significant, in fact, was the change he began to effect in himself that even his mother-in-law noticed it, and, for the first time in fifteen years, she began to look upon him differently, accept him, and stop carping about him to his wife. Coincidentally enough, her attacks of serious sickness also began to abate.

Meanwhile, as Mr. M was improving, I began to see his wife regularly. I had a fairly easy time of it with her, since she was most grateful, from the start, about what I had done to help her husband accept her and her mother. She admitted that her mother was difficult and that she herself was often put out by her tantrums. But she felt that she just had to keep catering to most of her mother's whims and she was now very happy that her husband had begun, at least partly, to see things her way and help abate the stressfulness of the situation.

As for Mr. M's allegiance to his own family, she still thought it *too* much. Again, as I usually do with my marriage counseling clients, I assumed that she was entirely right about his conventional adherence to his family's social functions, even though I already knew from talking to Mr. M, that he was not exactly that conventional, but kept up good social ties with his family because he wanted to ensure the possibility of getting a sizable inheritance from them. As I did with her husband, I showed Mrs. M that however wrong Mr. M might be in his dealings with his family, that was largely *his* problem, and there was no point in her making herself terribly disturbed about it.

"But doesn't his problem also involve me?" she objected. "Don't I have to go to these damned social affairs with him?"

"Certainly," I admitted, "his problem involves you to some extent. But not as much as you think it does. In the first place, you do *not* have to go to all the family affairs that he attends, but can frankly set, with him, a maximum number that you will attend a year, and stick to that maximum. That will make it all the more his problem if he insists on going to more than your maximum. Second, if you calm down and stop upsetting yourself *because* your husband presumably has a problem in this area, you will probably be able, two intelligent people like you, to work things out so as to minimize the effect of his problem on you. But if you continue to rant and rave, as you have been doing, instead of sitting down to a series of discussions about what to *do* about his problem, things will only get worse and worse—as they have been doing."

"That's for sure!"

"Right. So I'm not promising you any perfect solution to the problem, if you calm down and look at it *as* a problem. But at least, under those conditions there's a good chance that the two of you will come up with some kind of compromise solution. The way it is now, we get no solution, but only a continual worsening of the situation."

"But isn't it unfair that I have to be bothered by the fact that he has this problem and that I have to discuss it with him and make all kinds of compromises, when, really, he should just face the problem himself and get over it?"

"Let's suppose, for the sake of discussion, that it *is* unfair (although, actually, he could say to me that it's unfair that *you* do not see things his way and that *he* has to go to the trouble of compromising). Let's suppose that it's one hundred percent unfair to you that this kind of situation exists. Okay: so it's unfair. The world is full of all kinds of unfair things—of crooked politics, people starving to death while others live in luxury, and so on. And merely to cry and carp about its being that unfair is hardly going to help change things, is it? So if your husband is unfair in having this problem—which seems a little silly to say, doesn't it, since he hardly raised *himself* to have it—that's tough. As I said before: so it's 'unfair.'

"But the thing for *you* to do when faced with an unfair situation is: (a) try to unwhiningly change it, or (b) temporarily accept it as long as it can't for the moment be changed. And your crying and whining about how unfair the situation is are certainly not going to help you to do either (a) or (b). Are they?"

"No, I guess they aren't."

"All right," I said, "then when are you going to stop the non-sense—the nonsense, that is, that you keep feeding yourself? Granted that your husband may, as you say, have serious problems in regard to his family, but your problem is that you take his problem *too* seri-ously. Instead of understanding him and trying to help him *not* be so over-attached to his conventionalism, you are castigating him for his attachment—beating him over the head, as it were, for being too conformist. Will that help him be *less* conformist? Even if he is neu-rotically conformist, he probably became so because of being se-verely criticized by others and taking this criticism too much to heart. So will not your flagellating him help him become, if any-thing, *more* disturbed?"

"I see what you mean. What, specifically, then, should I do?"

"The same thing anyone can specifically do in a case like this, where an intimate associate is acting badly because of his own anxi-eties or hostilities. First, you can stop telling *yourself* how horrible his activities are. Second, you can accept him, for the time being, just because this is the way he is. Third, when you are calmly ac-cepting your husband's acts as *undesirable* but still not *horrible*, you can then ask yourself what you can do to help him feel more secure, so that he does not have to be so anxious or hostile. As we said be-fore, you can arrange various compromises, so that *you* do not have to be too badly affected even if, for the time being, he continues to act in much the same manner. In other words: the calmer you are and the more you stop giving yourself a hard time about your hus-band's behavior, the more chance you have of helping him change that behavior and of protecting yourself from the worst effects if he continues in much the same way. Does that give you a more specific idea of what you can do to try to help the present situation?"

"Yes, I think it does."

And, like her husband, Mrs. M did some tall talking to herself. She made herself less disturbed about her husband's participation in family affairs, and was able to show him understanding and help instead of carping and criticism. As a consequence, even though he still felt that it was desirable to keep seeing his family for economic reasons, he was able to compromise by seeing them less often and by frequently arranging to see them when his wife was not present. This former area of severe disagreement between Mr. and Mrs. M soon became no issue and they were able to spend much more of their time planning and engaging in more enjoyable aspects of life.

Can, in a similar manner, in-law problems be helped in other instances? To a great extent, yes. Almost always when there are serious in-law differences, the mates are disturbed because either their in-laws are not behaving in the way they think they *should* behave or their spouse is not acting toward these in-laws in the manner they think that s/he *must* act. Once the highly upset mates begin to question and challenge their own *shoulds*—rather than the behavior of their mate or in-laws—they almost immediately can begin to feel much better, less angry. And the better and less angry they feel, the greater, almost always, are their chances of doing something to improve the situation they abhor.

This is not to say that any husband or wife is not entitled to dislike the thoughts or actions of his or her spouse or in-laws. Dislike, yes—that is usually healthy. But when dislike is raised to severe hatred and continual backbiting, they foolishly add to the RB, "I wish this kind of behavior did not exist," the IB, "Because I wish this kind of behavior did not exist, it *should* not, *must* not exist!" This second belief is deadly. Tackling it—rather than tackling one's mate or in-laws—is a much better solution to this kind of problem.

In general, then, the line you can take to resolve serious disagreements that exist because of in-law difficulties may be as follows:

1. Accept your in-laws' shortcomings and/or your mate's "illogical" attitudes toward your in-laws as an undesirable but, for the time being, a largely unchangeable problem or annoyance.

2. Expect your in-laws and your spouse to act just the way they do, to be for the present just the way they are, and stop telling yourself that it is awful, terrible, and frightful that they act this way.

3. Do not personalize your in-laws' behavior toward you. Even if they are vicious, unfair, and thoroughly unreasonable, that is *their* problem and has nothing intrinsically to do with you. If they hate you, that does not make *you* a hateful person. If they are obstreperous or interfering, that does not make *you* weak. Cultivate your own garden, and take care of your own thoughts and feelings, and there is very little that they can actually do to make you disturbed.

4. By all means, if feasible, do not live too close to your in-laws. You can arrange to see them relatively infrequently, and avoid living in the same apartment house, or even neighborhood, with them if you can help it. But if you must, for some reason, see them relatively often, do not think that being with them, in, of, and by itself need be harmful. The worst they can do, normally, is act nastily toward you or call you names. Too bad! Does it make *that* much difference? What can they really *do* to you?

5. Once you understand your in-laws and their problems, by all means try to help them change for the better, if you can. But don't *expect* them to change because you *want* them to. And try to honestly see their point of view, be on their side, help them for their own sake as well as your own. Don't try to change them by criticism, carping, grim silence, or persecution. Try to *help* them change, do not blackmail or force them into changing.

6. Don't allow yourself to be exploited, physically or emotionally, by your in-laws just because you *are* related to them. You owe them: (a) normal human politeness, and (b) acknowledgment of the fact that they are the parents of your spouse, and that for his/her sake you will try to be as pleasant as possible to them. But you are not obligated to give them your complete allegiance, perform acts of extreme self-sacrifice for them, or go dramatically against your own grain. If you cannot get along well with them you can, without being downright unpleasant, calmly but firmly divorce yourself emotionally from them—and thus even, perhaps, set a good example for your spouse. But if s/he still wants to be very closely tied to your in-laws, you can calmly accept these ties, for the nonce, while intelligently and lovingly trying to deal with her.

7. If your in-laws, in spite of everything you can do, insist on re-

maining a thorn in your side and are truly obnoxious, and if you cannot keep them from unduly influencing your spouse, you must philosophically accept the fact that conditions in this respect are *bad*—but that, again, they are not necessarily *horrible* and *awful.* Perhaps you cannot reduce your annoyance at your in-laws' behavior but you can at least stop yourself from needlessly making yourself utterly miserable about it.

8. There is no law against your liking your in-laws and actually getting along very well with them. Particularly if you do not take them too seriously, if you realistically accept their limitations, and if you do not expect them to be perfect or act exceptionally well to you, you may find that they are quite decent, helpful, nice enough people with whom you have some things in common and can get along very pleasantly in many ways. They did, after all, bear and rear your spouse, who presumably has some really nice qualities, and it is most unlikely that they are complete ogres. The better you accept yourself, the less you personalize their views of you, and the more philosophical you are about many of life's irritations and annoyances, the more are you likely to find excellent points in your in-laws and to be able to enjoy them in important respects.

Again, as ever, we teach one main thing in this book: that almost all your severe emotional problems are your *own. You* have the ability to disturb or not disturb yourself, therefore—whatever problems your in-laws and their relationship with your spouse may seem to create. Your attitude toward these troubles, rather than the difficulties in themselves, will determine whether you are quite miserable or satisfied with your marriage and your life.

EXERCISES FOR CHAPTER 9

You may be fortunate enough to have a partner but not have in-laws or other close relatives of this partner. Maybe they have all died, live in Alaska, or hate social contact. Fine! Or maybe they are quite likable, a pleasure to be with. Marvelous!

If not, here are some exercises you can use to help cope with your partner's close relatives. Or, if they're no problem, perhaps you can use these exercises to bear up under the strain of dealing with your mate's annoying close friends or business associates. To some extent, these exercises probably apply to various restrictions and hassles of mating and relating. If they don't, bless your luck and skip them!

One of REBT's most useful emotive-evocative methods, which I (Dr. Ellis) developed in the 1970s, is the vigorous and forceful disputing of people's IBs. I found that a number of my resistant clients were competently disputing their IBs and coming up with sensible, rational effective new philosophies (Es) but that they only mildly or lightly believed them, and wound up with mild Es. Their quite powerful and forceful IBs, which they still held, unfortunately won out—to their great emotional loss.

So I give many of my clients the homework assignments of putting some of their IBs on a tape recorder, of very vigorously disputing these IBs, of letting their IBs and their disputing be heard by friends or group members, and of then revising their disputing, if necessary, and making it more powerful and convincing. We find this to be a useful disputing method. You can use it as follows.

Sample Exercise 9A: Vigorous and Forceful Disputing of My IBs About Dealing With My Partner's Relatives

My Irrational Beliefs That I Can Vigorously Dispute	Vigorous Disputation of My IBs	Strong Effective New Philosophies (Es)
Some of my partner's relatives are so obnoxious that I certainly shouldn't have to socialize with them.	Are they really *that* obnoxious or am *I* grossly exaggerating? Even if I'm right about them is there really *any* reason why I *absolutely shouldn't have to* socialize with them?	*Yes, I am* grossly exaggerating how obnoxious they are! *No matter!* However bad they are, that's the way they are! I *should* have to socialize with them if I desire to have good relationships with my mate! Being with them is bad—but being without my mate is *much, much worse! Tough turkey* if they bore me! *I can take it!*
My mate's parents really *are* rotten people! I can't find *anything* good about them. Murder is too good for them!	Are they *completely* rotten people or do they just do *some* rotten things? Isn't my raging at them *also* silly and rotten?	*No one* is completely rotten—not even them and Hitler! I'm idiotically damning *them* and not just their *behavior! Yes,* I'm ridiculously incensing myself at them and ripping up my own gut. What drivel!
Look how needy my partner is—putting up with lousy relatives like that. S/he *needs* their ass-kissing ap-	Is my partner needy—or just really appreciative of his or her relatives? Even if s/he is needy, is that utterly	How about *my* neediness?—my *demand* that my partner have the "right" relatives? It's *good* that s/he can

Exercise 9A (cont.)

My Irrational Beliefs That I Can Vigorously Dispute	Vigorous Disputation of My IBs	Strong Effective New Philosophies (Es)
proval. How disgusting! I'll show him/her how revolting that is!	*disgusting? Must* I show him/her how revolting that behavior is?	find value in people that I am bigotedly condemning entirely. I am foolishly revolting *myself*. And *I'm* the one who's stupidly making myself suffer and disrupting my relationship! How revolting is *that*!

Exercise 9B: Vigorous and Forceful Disputing of My IBs About Dealing With My Partner's Relatives

My Irrational Beliefs That I Can Vigorously Dispute	My Vigorous Disputations of These Irrational Beliefs

Exercise 9C: Role-Playing About My Upsetness About My Partner's Relatives

REBT often uses J.L. Moreno's role-play exercise to help people overcome their needless upset feelings and to learn better social skills. Thus, if you are angry or overly frustrated about your partner's relatives, friends, or associates, enlist a friend to help you cope with your disturbed feelings and to train yourself to act better with your partner and his/her "terrible" associates. You play yourself during the role-play and your friend can play your mate. Your goal is to practice speaking *assertively* but not *angrily* to your partner. Thus, your role-play dialogue may go as follows:

You: I know it's your father's birthday, dear, but you know he's not exactly my cup of tea. So you can see him as long as you like, but do I really have to be there, too?

Your Mate: Oh! But he and Mom will be terribly hurt if you don't come with me. They'll know you really hate him.

You: Maybe you're right, dear. But I really don't hate him. I just hate some of the ways he acts.

Your Mate: But they'll be sure you hate him. And they'll think you also don't respect me.

You: Of course I respect and love you. And I wouldn't want to keep you from seeing your father if you really want to do so.

Your Mate: If you really loved me, you wouldn't put me in this position. You'd go, even though you don't like it.

You: I can see how you see it that way. But I *do* love you. I just hate hearing him go on and on as he usually does. None of us get a word in edgewise!

Your Mate: He's not that bad! And you'd still do it for me. You know how it would hurt me to go alone.

You: Yes, and I want to avoid that. Now couldn't we compromise? Couldn't I go for only a short while and then plead an important business appointment? We could even call them in advance and tell them I can only visit briefly.

Your Mate: Lie like that? I'd hate to make up a lie like that.

Exercise 9C (cont.)

You: Yes, so would I. But wouldn't it be, dear, the lesser of evils? And, to make things better, I could even buy him an expensive gift—like a special golf club he would like—to show him that I really like him.

Your Mate: Well—?

In a role-play like this, you work at not making yourself angry at your partner and arriving at some kind of compromise. Your role-playing friend—and other possible onlookers—critique your performance, tell you how to improve it, and get you to replay it until you do improve. If you appear to be angry, depressed, anxious, or otherwise disturbed during the role-play, stop it for a few minutes to see what you are telling yourself to make yourself upset and how you can change your self-talk to reduce your disturbance.

Thus, in the previous dialogue, if your partner said, "Lie like that? I'd hate to make up a lie like that," and you then felt anxious, the two of you—and other possible onlookers—would stop to ask, "What are you telling yourself to make yourself anxious?"

You might reply, "My partner is putting me down for suggesting that we lie. Right! I'm a lousy liar—and a no-goodnik!"

You and your partner would dispute this IB and might come up with the Effective New Philosophy that lying may indeed be bad but it never makes you a *bad person*. Then you could continue the role-play.

So again: If you really are upset about your partner's having "miserable" relatives, friends, or associates, you can use this REBT version of role-playing to retain your displeasure, but reduce your upsetness and function better with your partner and/or his or her "rotten" associates.

10

To Have or Not to Have Children—That *Is* the Question

While few people think they can, without much preparation and training, fly a jet plane, teach a course in nuclear physics or reprogram a bevy of complex computers, we keep running into hordes who not only think they themselves are naturally destined to be dandy parents, but also that others less magnificently endowed than themselves can easily and automatically undertake the glories of parenthood and turn out super-duper children. All you have to do to get an A-plus in parenting, they insist, is to be properly and legally married, for all husbands and wives—of course—are born with superlative child-raising skills and are able to bear incredibly marvelous offspring. If you sorely lack such skills, well, take a chance, anyway. What have you and your brats got to lose? As the Bible brilliantly proclaims, "Be fruitful and multiply."

Are we being sarcastic? In a word, yes. For we would like to highlight some of the common irrationalities of our society about children and parenthood. There are loads of such IBs. Even though large numbers of people hold that reproduction is to be encouraged and that child-rearing is a process for which no great knowledge or skill is needed, couples who want to *adopt* children usually have to meet fairly strict standards. These standards are often difficult to measure and/or fulfill. Couples must, for example, somehow demonstrate present and future happiness and emotional and financial stability. Couples who reveal themselves to be too old or too young, perhaps homosexual, or different from arbitrarily predetermined "desirable" social or religious philosophies are often eliminated.

Our stance as a society on a couple's acquiring children seems to be: if you do it by reproduction, "feel free (but please be married)." If by adoption, "Hey, wait a minute, we are very concerned about the kind of parents and the kind of environment this child will have." We would expand considerably on prevalent attitudes about having children, but we hope we've said enough or at least cast doubt on the rationality and realism of what seems to be our society's position.

It is not the purpose of this chapter to join society in trying to persuade "a nice young married couple" that they ought or ought not to have children. All couples have the right to choose—rationally or irrationally—*not* to become parents just as they have the right to decide not to work for the government or to live in a large city or to buy an automobile. With the help of this chapter, work out the important factors in your particular situation in deciding whether or not to be parents. Let us pose some questions and hazard some "rational" or "healthy" answers—for some of our readers some of the time!

Question: Is it essential to our happiness and welfare for us to have children?

Answer: It all depends. Are you sure that you can't be happy without children or that you would be happy with children? Have all your relatives been really happy with their children? And what about their children—do they all seem top-ho? What about the background, skills, and attitudes you are both bringing into this deal? Aren't those the sort of questions your partner and you should preferably be discussing at great length?

Question: What are some important things to consider in deciding whether to have or not have children? Shall we have them just because we are happy with each other?

Answer: Probably not. Your being happy together is a good sign but hardly a *demand* for your having children. Would having them help or hinder your relationship? Hmm . . . Is your marriage the kind of process that a kid will fit into and enjoy (let alone your enjoying the kid)? Or is your relationship one of those great me-thee things that leave little room for *anybody* else?

Question: How about my partner and us *liking* children and *being good* with them?

Answer: A good question. We remember a botany teacher who said he loved his children and that they loved him. But he loved it even more when he could walk away and leave the responsibility of them to his wife and to other people. We used to think he was just a funny guy whose words had no great importance. But don't they? Shouldn't you and your partner think of ways of testing whether you like kids and will get along with them well on a long-term basis? Would you be willing to provide foster home care for a while? And what does it say about having a child of your own if one or both of you isn't willing?

Question: Do we really have sufficient time together to properly raise children?

Answer: Perhaps. But don't forget that these days, with both mates often employed outside the home, a lot of couples have insufficient time together *without* children. Think carefully! What are you now doing that you would have to greatly reduce to properly raise children.

Question: Will our ideas and interests about having children change *after* we actually have them?

Answer: They well may! Jim got all fired up about being a stock broker, studied like mad, passed all the tests, had the highest sales record for several months. Then his interest fizzled. He thought, "So I make a lot of money. So I help other dopes make a lot of money. So who cares? It's a bore." Mary loved teaching third grade for three years—then hated it and became a happy paralegal. How can you and your partner really know how much, after a while, you will adore your own children? Not very easily!

Question: Now with all our doubt and confusion, do we just give up on having children?

Answer: Not necessarily. There's a long road to go before the *two* of you decide about having children. But you'd better get out of that children-are-my-destiny mood and be ready to work at deciding what you and your partner think is an intelligent decision. Yes, *work* at deciding.

These questions and answers were condensed from discussions we have had with individuals and couples through the years on the issues of having children. As therapists, we never try to persuade one way or the other. But since the weight of society has often pushed couples directly into parenthood, we encourage careful consideration of the problems of parenthood. If and when a couple determines to have a child we try to help them undertake parenthood realistically and to enjoy it fully.

Once a couple decides to have a child, we often make the following points. But these, like everything else in this book, are subject to discussion and revision by any specific couple.

1. While love is definitely not "all that matters," and certainly need not meet some special forms of expressions, partners A and B had better deeply and consistently care for each other and for their children.

2. They had better strive for both short-range and (especially) long-range enjoyment. They also had better include in their enjoyments working at improving interactions and responsibilities in their family.

3. They had better expect and accept their own and their children's mistakes and limitations. Their unperfectionistic outlooks will appreciably reduce anger, anxiety, and other strong disruptive emotions that often develop in close human relationships.

4. They had better teach their children how to minimize their mistakes and learn from them.

5. They had better acknowledge that the knowledge and skills most people bring to parenthood leave plenty of room for improvement. Just as we have noted in earlier chapters, improved family functioning usually can be achieved only by careful assessment, planned discussion, and hard work at improving family members' disturbed habits of thinking, feeling, and acting.

6. Couples had better recognize the individuality of their children. This means gradually relinquishing their control over their offspring and encouraging them to increasingly participate in decisions that affect the whole family unit.

EXERCISES FOR CHAPTER 10

The main problems concerning children that we keep encountering with our clients include:

Serious disagreements over whether or not to have them.

Disagreements over whether to have additional children.

Disagreements over how to raise the children the couple actually have.

Disagreements over whether to keep supporting the children when they have already reached adulthood.

As with other relationship disagreements you have, your problem with your partner is not so much to agree but to agree to disagree— to disagree amiably. As usual, the chief block here is, first, too much pride, which leads to self-downing.

Janis, for example, fought bitterly with Jim over whether they should have a child, even though she was highly ambivalent about bearing one at the age of thirty-nine and he was positive that having one would be a "huge mistake." But she felt that if he wouldn't even *consider* her mild wish to have a child he had no respect for her as a *person*. She viewed her giving in to him, even when she was convinced she was right, as a "terrible weakness." So she "strongly" kept fighting with Jim until she almost proved to be infertile. After she became pregnant, she still resented his previous "pigheadedness" and tended to "find" it in other respects where it really did not exist.

Exercise 10A is useful when you and your mate keep violently disagreeing about children or anything else because one or both of you cannot bear being "weak" by compromising. It is also useful when the main reason for your disagreement is your low frustration tolerance. Thus, Jim kept fighting with Janis against their having a child because he knew he would enjoy one later but horrified himself about the loss of sleep and other inconveniences he and Janis would experience for the first year or two of the child's life. When he worked on his LFT and decided to put up with this rough period of time, he was quite happy for the rest of his life about having a charming, bright daughter.

In the following exercise, you will be making a list of the advantages and the disadvantages of arguing with your mate to prove that you are not a weak person or to uphold your LFT. Rate or evaluate each of these advantages from a low of one to a high of ten, especially in terms of enhancing and of sabotaging your relationship.

Sample Exercise 10A: Mapping Out the Cost-Benefit Ratio of Arguing With Your Mate to Prove That You Are Not a "Weak Person" or to Uphold Your LFT

Advantages of Maintaining Strong Arguments With Partner	Rating of Advantages	Disadvantages of Maintaining Strong Arguments with Partner	Rating of Disadvantages
I feel like a strong person when I stubbornly hold my ground.	7	I may argue strongly but am I not really weak for *needing* to win?	10
My friends and relatives will like me for strongly holding my ground.	3	I will have more strength if I don't need my friends' and relatives' approval.	8
If I disagree about having another child, we will save a lot of money.	8	If I disagree about having a child, I will lose out on the excitement, love, and enjoyment of agreeing to have one.	8
People will look down on me for being childless so I have to keep fighting with my mate to have a child andperhaps two or three children. I must not be criticized for being childless.	5	If I agree with my mate that we don't have children and we are criticized for being childless, I can still accept myself fully in spite of people's criticism	9

Exercise 10A

Advantages of Maintaining Strong Arguments With Partner	Rating of Advantages	Disadvantages of Maintaining Strong Arguments With Partner	Rating of Disadvantages

If you want, you can total up your ratings for the advantages and disadvantages of maintaining strong arguments with your partner—and hope that you view the disadvantages as greater and thereby give yourself incentives for making compromises and resisting continual arguments.

Sample Exercise 10B: Advantages and Disadvantages of My Partner and I Possibly Rearing Children

As in the previous exercise, you may rate each advantage and each disadvantage you expect to receive from rearing children from one to ten and see which side comes out with a higher rating. This kind of cost-benefit rating—or hedonic calculus—may be an important factor in which you or your mate decide whether or not to have children.

Advantages My Partner and I Will Probably Experience If We Rear Children	Rating of Advantages	Disadvantages My Partner and I Will Probably Experience If We Rear Children	Rating of Disadvantages
Monetary advantages, such as becoming forced to budget and save money. The self-discipline you may achieve by raising children.		The expenses you will have with your children. The time and energy you will probably spend in raising children.	
The love you will feel for your children.		The anger and LFT you may feel with your children.	
The love your children will feel toward you and your partner.		The selfishness your children may exhibit toward you and your partner.	
The fine companionship you may have with your children.		The lack of companionship you may have with your children or the too-great responsibilities you may feel about being with them.	
The interesting experiences you may have with your children.		The boredom you may experience with your children.	

Exercise 10B

Advantages My Partner and I Will Probably Experience If We Rear Children	Rating of Advantages	Disadvantages My Partner and I Will Probably Experience If We Rear Children	Rating of Disadvantages
_____	_____	_____	_____
_____	_____	_____	_____
_____	_____	_____	_____
_____	_____	_____	_____
_____	_____	_____	_____
_____	_____	_____	_____
_____	_____	_____	_____
_____	_____	_____	_____
_____	_____	_____	_____
_____	_____	_____	_____
_____	_____	_____	_____
_____	_____	_____	_____
_____	_____	_____	_____

11

Happy Couplehood: Building a Deep and Lasting Relationship

Throughout this book, we have held that if you and your partner persistently apply the basic tenets of REBT, you can help yourself to long-term enjoyment of living. We have also pointed out the advantages you have, as a couple, of developing and testing out the revolutionary REBT ways of thinking, feeling, and acting. Moreover, this application can be nicely mixed with fun. Put somewhat differently, the REBT route to lasting happy relating is hard work, but the hard work itself can be a process of fun, and the fun itself can be greatly enhanced by having a partner to work and play with.

In this last chapter we want to help bring out some general points about couplehood, and we fortunately have the help of an old friend. Do you remember Charlene, the fifteen-year-old who was so distressed about her lesbian tendencies? Let us go further along with her saga by taking a look at interviews with Charlene and her partner, Nita, which took place eight years after the conversations with her reported in chapter one.

Charlene: Yes, it's been almost eight fucking years since I saw you. I'm twenty-three now, and about to get a Ph.D in psychology from (she named a local university). You're responsible for that: you not only cured me of self-downing, but you got me fascinated with clinical psychology. I tried heterosexuality, by the way. In fact you might say I gave going straight a hell of a case, but I always got back to the proposition that this ain't me and there is no damned reason why it has to be me. I've had several brief affairs with other women, but Nita is the first person with whom I've ever felt I wanted to have a lasting relationship. She feels similarly about me. I don't want to blow this, and that's why we're here. I think that I've really lived sensibly as an individual, but I could use REBT more in an ongoing relationship.

R.A.H.: If you have been applying REBT in the rest of your life, you'll find that there is nothing amazingly different about applying it in a close personal relationship. In fact, there are various advantages, providing that both partners are willing to work in the REBT mode. What about you, Nita?

Nita: Yeah, well, I'm a little overwhelmed—first of all because Charlene is older and more experienced. I'm just nineteen and a first-semester junior and only beginning my psychology major. And she's not only a hotshot graduate student, but she's also this super-dynamo, Charlene. Then she drags me in here to see you after having talked about you for months as if you were the living Christ. I feel like a walk-on bit player who's having lunch with the two stars of the play. But let's continue.

Charlene: You have no damned business being overwhelmed. I wouldn't have brought you here if I didn't think you were great!

R.A.H.: Several important things have just emerged that I'd like to suggest that the two of you look at: (1) Nita is understandably ill at ease in this situation and picked her own way of expressing it, (2) Instead of letting Nita work out her nervousness (with help from me if necessary), you, Charlene, told her in effect that she has no damned business being "overwhelmed," and (3) It's interesting that you presumably tried to reassure Nita that I am an okay person rather than demonstrating what would seem more pertinent—that you, Charlene, accept Nita in what she finds to be a difficult situation. You both seem to know how desirable *acceptance* is but you are hardly displaying it. Let's try an REBT exercise. Will you both close your eyes, please? Now will each of you, keeping your eyes closed, honestly look at the negative feelings you have about each other. Don't think in terms of what you suspect the other is going to report, but get in touch with your own feelings. Focus on what you feel and not on any justification you can produce for feeling that way.

(After a minute or so.) Okay, Nita first. What did you recognize in the way of negative feelings toward Charlene? Please, both of you keep your eyes closed while Nita is talking. You'll get your chance later, Charlene.

Nita: I feel that Charlene thinks I'm inferior. Cute, but dumb. And I hate her for that. But I also feel she is conning herself into believing that she wants a long-term relationship (and that's why we are in here), when what she really wants is to sex it up with me like mad and tell herself it's beautiful love. I hate that even more, but my hate toward Charlene about that is less than it is about the cute-but-dumb theme. I also feel hostility toward myself and that sort of spills over onto Charlene because I'm such a wimp and suck up to Charlene because she's Ms. Hotshot. My hostility toward Charlene and toward myself is further reinforced by Ms. Hotshot telling me, even in here, what I'm supposed to think and feel.

R.A.H.: That's fine. Now keeping your eyes closed (both of you), see if you, Nita, can changes these feelings into less disturbed and more positive ones. Please both be silent, and Nita, hold up your hand when you are ready to report. In the meantime, please be patient, Charlene. (After three minutes Nita holds up her hand.) Okay, will you both continue with closed eyes please, and Nita will you tell us what you *now* feel and, if your feelings are different, how you changed them?

Nita: It's funny, but I feel quite different. I believed up to now that REBT was largely bullshit, especially the part about how I can feel differently by thinking differently. I thought my feelings were my essence—that I feel as I feel because I am as I am. Charlene was always telling me that was a lot of crap, but I would react defensively because she *told* me to feel different. Just now, because I felt okay feeling any damned hostile way I wanted and because I was simply given an opportunity to change in case *I* wanted to do so, I did want to.

R.A.H.: How did you do it? And how do you know you are not just bullshitting yourself in some new way?

Nita: I think the main way I did it was by wanting to look realistically at what I was feeling and why. When I started looking, I started thinking, and when I started thinking I came up with the idea, which gradually became a feeling: Hey, Nita, all this defensiveness and hostility is for the birds. And I came up next with the idea that I don't have to measure up to some kind of standard that I think Charlene has set for me. I've got problems to work out, but I'm an okay person even if I don't work them out. And what's more, it won't be terrible if Charlene's and my relationship doesn't become the lasting and beautiful thing we've talked about. And how do I know I am not bullshitting myself in a new way? I guess I don't *know*, but I think the probability is that I'm thinking clearer and I'm certainly feeling better. At least it's a better-quality bullshit!

R.A.H.: Yes, it sounds as if you embraced at least two important ideas. First, you don't have to meet predetermined standards to be an acceptable person. Second, even if you don't solve your problems or work out a desirable relationship with Charlene, although I assume that is still your preference (Nita: Yes!), life won't be terrible. That's considerable progress. But let's now give Charlene her chance. Will you both please continue to keep your eyes closed, so that you keep focused. You have undoubtedly reacted to some of the things that Nita said, Charlene. So will you try as best you can to tell us what your own thinking and feeling processes have been?

Charlene: It was good to hear Nita's "yes" about wanting still to work out our relationship. I had thought I'd blown it to hell. And though I have, of course, been listening to what Nita and you have been saying, I had already looked at my thoughts and feelings and how they needed to be changed—oh, I'm sorry, not *needed*, but *had better* be changed. You see, I remember many of the lessons I learned from you in REBT years ago. And I practiced these things, and they helped me to function better and to do well in many respects and to enjoy myself along the way. *But* Nita sure as hell is right. I began to think of myself as a hotshot who could do no wrong and whose point of view was always fucking right. Anyone who disagreed with me was either a hopeless pain in the ass and therefore to be dismissed—or was a fine person, Nita being the prime example, who had to be shown the way and the light by wonderful me. I now know that I have been behaving like an asshole, but I have enough REBT left in me to know that it doesn't mean I *am* an asshole. I'm an okay person who has been *behaving* assholishly! And I am going to fucking stop behaving like that!

R.A.H.: Can you help Nita and me to understand better what got you off the REBT track? Incidentally, both of you can open your eyes now.

Charlene: Well, mostly success. I remember something back in a psychoanalytic seminar which said that the neurotic may fail because of the fear of success. But my own experience is you fail by *corrupting* success. The more I succeeded the more I came to believe I was a top-ho who *couldn't* fail. I believed what you stressed with me years ago, that REBT works *only* if we work at it, applied only to the average stiff and not to a queen of the shitpile like me. And, you know, my experience in therapy training as well as my razzle-dazzle success in graduate school added to my belief that I could walk on water. Many clients are so grateful for any kind of help that they treat a two-bit therapist like a guru and it's easy to come to believe that you actually are one. Anyhow, it's easy to spout REBT to clients and to forget to practice it oneself. Then there are all these other kinds of therapies that distracted me from keeping the old REBT nose to the grindstone. Anyhow, even though I was going around spouting REBT principles to everybody, including Nita, I was getting more and more off the REBT practicing track. I think I'm now ripe for more personal help as well as doing my part in couple therapy.

R.A.H.: There isn't all that much difference between doing your part in couple therapy and getting some personal help. You describe well some of the hazards of therapists getting off the personal practicing of REBT. That's why, you'll recall, I kept stressing years ago that living the REBT way takes constant vigilance and unremitting hard work.

Charlene: Yes, I remember, and I worked hard at it for a long while. But I guess I began gradually to believe that it was automatic with me, and I would just naturally do the most rational and healthy thing. And I extended my conceit to Nita's and my relationship with her, and assumed that I was so wonderful that any relationship she had with me was bound to be great and beautiful. When it hasn't worked out that way, I've blamed Nita. She, I'd think and all too often say, was being obstinate or stupid or unappreciative or some damned thing. So, she's right. I decided to haul her in here so you could give her a quick fix.

R.A.H.: In any close relationship, it's common—but unproductive—to blame the partner for any difficulty that develops. Blame is not only non-acceptance of the partner, but it arouses your mate's defensiveness, blame, and non-acceptance. This, in turn, elicits more of the same, on and on. When you seem to be falling into this sort of pattern, try using the eyes-closed exercise you just experienced here. You can give yourselves instructions like these: "We have a problem. Let's each of us focus on what each of us (*not* the other one) can do to alleviate it." Later, you can describe to one another where each of you sees herself as being "off-track" and what she can do to correct it.

Nita: Is it that easy? A little eye-closing exercise, and Charlene and I will achieve beautiful bliss?

R.A.H.: No, Nita, you have just illustrated two common false assumptions about REBT. For one, you assumed that because some of its therapy instructions are simple, REBT is easy. For example, if I say, "If you want to develop real proficiency in understanding and speaking Aleut, you will probably have to seek out and study with an Aleutian," it does not mean I think it would be *easy* to do this. Second, you assumed that using REBT for alleviating problems is the same as saying, "All my problems will be solved. Beautiful bliss is at hand." But we have more to do in REBT than eye-closing exercises. Charlene, you said at the outset that you had been trying to live in an REBT way as an individual, but knew little about applying it in a couple relationship. Do you want to say anything about that at this point?

Charlene: Seriously, in spite of how I just screwed up with Nita, I have really been living REBT. I've been preaching it to her while engaging in some anti-REBT rating of myself as a person. Something I've just faced today, in rating myself top-ho as a *person*, rather than rating my good behavior, I end up as far removed from the REBT way of life as I did when I rated myself as a lowly shit. So I have been ignoring REBT in my relationship with Nita. But I was talking bullshit about not knowing how to apply it to a close personal relationship. That was an excuse to myself to get Nita and me here. But we also genuinely had reason to get here because I, at least, had become confused.

Nita: (to Charlene) Your even admitting that you're confused is a new experience for me, and I like it. You seem much more available for democratic problem-solving than I have ever noticed before. (to me) I'm beginning to see what focusing can do. My sarcastic remarks earlier were, I think, partly from being *told* what to do by Charlene. I made myself over-react to that.

R.A.H.: I'm glad that you see that it was *your* over-reacting and not merely Charlene's trying to tell you what to do. Both of you can, I hope, now understand that the eyes-closed routine helps you to focus more intently on acknowledging and (sometimes) changing your thoughts and feelings. But there's no reason why enlightenment *must* invariably proceed in that fashion. If Charlene lapses into her old dictatorial habits from time to time, you can realize that she is working on reducing this tendency and you can work on being less vulnerable to it. Correct?

This first couples session with Charlene and Nita kept repeating some of the above points, but to make my points clearer, much repetition is omitted here. Remember, however, it is important to remember in your own discussions with your partner—and perhaps with your therapist—that you seldom effect change without going over and over the same "simple and easy" matters almost monotonously! Comments made by Charlene, Nita, and myself in the remainder of this chapter have been excerpted from eight subsequent sessions.

Nita: At home, things go a little more smoothly than in these sessions. But what we find works best is for one or both of us to say something like, "Hey, we seem to have a problem here. Let's pause, close our eyes, and try to understand what each of us is thinking and feeling and how we might improve it." Both the pause and the self-focusing seem helpful.

Charlene: You asked our permission to use some of the things the three of us say in these sessions in a book on helping couples that you are writing. Do you really think problems of couples are the same whether they are straight, gay, rednecks, dope addicts, or devoted members of religious sects?

R.A.H.: Partly. The particular content and seriousness of problems will vary with the characteristics and circumstances of the individuals who are paired. To have a leg amputated would obviously be a much more serious problem for a professional hockey player than for an accountant, and therefore also more serious for the hockey player's partner. Yet, *how* the two *approach* and *handle* their problems can determine the hockey player and his partner's ending up in a better long-term relationship than an accountant and his or her mate. REBT tries to offer couples (and individuals) more effective ways of dealing with *whatever* problems they encounter. So although all couples hardly have the same problems, most of them can learn to handle their difficulties and differences more wisely. I think a straight couple, for example, could just as well apply some of the things we have discussed in our sessions as could another lesbian couple.

Nita: Let me ask something at this point. I know you helped Charlene to work through the lesbian issue when she was just a kid, but she still had some doubts in recent years and I do, too. Aren't we *realistically* adding to our other life problems by insisting on a lesbian lifestyle? Women are already discriminated against in society,

so when two women get together and thumb their noses at tradi-
tional values, aren't they just dipping into deep shit?

R.A.H.: No, not necessarily. As lesbians in our prejudiced culture, you just have another set of difficulties to realistically consider.
Even with all the usual couple problems and, with a set of unusual
additional ones, you can still be happy. I have worked with people
who had all kinds of handicaps and problems but who have learned
through REBT to take them in stride. Many others catastrophize
over a late plane or train, over their coworker's jealousy, and over
innumerable other "petty" things.

Despite your doubts, you and Charlene have made the practical
decision to function as lesbians. Why do you make this choice? No
one precisely knows. Can you reverse your decision if you are really
determined to do so? Possibly, but Charlene at age fifteen was determined not to do so and neither of you show determination now.
You both just have doubts now and then, which will probably get
you nowhere. So *practically*, let's focus on the hard work you can do
to function effectively and enjoyably together.

Charlene: How much do we have to do by rote the various exercises for couples you have taught us? How much do these procedures vary from those you use with other couples? I am interested as
a budding therapist who would like to some day do couple therapy.

R.A.H.: Let me give you an imprecise answer. REBT practitioners do better when they avoid procedures that are too fixed and me-
chanical. They try to adapt their methods to specific personalities
and situations. And they enlist aid from the couples themselves.
The mates know each other and can often assist with more spon-
taneity and creativity than can a single client who just interacts with
a therapist. REBT-oriented individual and couple therapy are different—and also similar! Both are fascinating.

Charlene: Is this, then, termination? Are you going to turn Nita
and me out into the hostile fucking world? Aren't you going to kiss
and hug us? There would be no trouble with the American Psycho-
logial Association ethics committee, because both Nita and I will
testify that you demonstrate no lesbian tendencies.

R.A.H.: Yes, but suppose I get hauled on the carpet for harassing you to try heterosexuality! No. For the present, you're on your own—to use, or to not use, REBT as you will. If you screw up, give yourselves unconditional self-acceptance and give each other unconditional other-acceptance and get back to working things out. If and when the going gets rough, remember the famous words of REBT: "Tough shit!" Good luck—and hard work—to both of you!

12

Summary: How You Can Use REBT to Build a Healthy Relationship

We have presented in this book many of the principles and practices of REBT, as well as suggestions on how to use them in your relationship. Let us briefly sum up our main suggestions.

First, rid yourself of the almost universal idea that your partner, by his or her "bad" behavior, upsets you. This is only partly true! Mainly, you can *take* your partner's undesirable thoughts, feelings, and actions and consciously or unconsciously upset yourself *about* them. As we say in REBT, the adversities of your life, A, may *significantly* contribute to your disturbed consequences, C, but you importantly *add* definite beliefs, B, *about* you and your partner's "wrong" actions to make yourself wind up with upset feelings and dysfunctional behaviors. A times B equals C!

This is fortunate. Because as constructivists, you and your partner have the power to construct and to reconstruct your own *reactions* to "bad" events that occur in your life. You can therefore sometimes change serious adversities themselves, and you can just about always change how you react (well or badly) to them. You can, at point B, construct both self-helping RBs and self-defeating IBs to difficulties in your relationships. RBs, as opposed to IBs, take the form of your *preferences* that adversities be reduced—for example, "I don't *like* my partner's behavior and *wish* s/he would change it. But, if not, we can still have a satisfying relationship." IBs take the form of you and/or your partner's absolutistic, rigid demands—e.g., "Because I don't like my partner's behavior, s/he *absolutely must not* think, feel, or act that way! If so, it's *awful* (totally bad) and s/he is a *rotten person!*"

Using REBT helps you to clearly see your irrational *demands* on yourself, your partner, and the world, and to change them back to rational *preferences*. As this book shows, it gives you many cognitive, emotional-experiential, and behavioral techniques for doing so. It emphasizes that you and your partner often hold IBs *strongly* (emotionally) and *actively* (behaviorally) and therefore it helps both of you emotionally and behaviorally, as well as cognitively, to see and surrender your IBs and your consequent dysfunctioning.

Most partners who get themselves into trouble with themselves and with others make one, two, or three major irrational, dysfunctional demands. If you often disturb yourself and contribute to disturbing your partner, REBT shows you ways to think, feel, and act against these demands and to acquire three important constructive philosophies that can help you enormously to stop wrecking your relationship and build a lasting, loving one. These are:

Unconditional other-acceptance (UOA). Accepting, respecting, honoring, and loving your partner (and other people) even *with* his/her shortcomings and failings. Strongly seeing and feeling the Christian idea of accepting the sinner but not the sin. Despite all!

Unconditional self-acceptance (USA). Accepting your self, essence, totality, and being *whether or not* you act well and *whether or not* you are approved of by significant others. Under all conditions!

Unconditional life-acceptance (ULA) or high frustration tolerance. Accepting life with its hassles, problems, troubles, and difficulties, and creating enjoyment in it for yourself and your partner. Not always, but fairly consistently!

These are our main REBT suggestions. By all means consider and *experiment* flexibly with them. You and your partner are unique individuals. Uniquely, as a person and as a couple, experiment with these REBT methods for yourself. Once again: Good luck—and hard work—to both of you!

Suggested Reading

The following references include a number of REBT and Cognitive Behavior Therapy publications which may be useful for self-help purposes. Many of these materials can be obtained from the Albert Ellis Institute, 45 East 65th Street, New York, N.Y. 10021-6593. The Institute's free catalog may be ordered on weekdays by phone (212-535-0822), by fax (212-249-3582) or by e-mail (orders@rebt.org).

Alberti, R. and Emmons, R. (1995). *Your Perfect Right.* 7th ed. San Luis Obispo, Cal.: Impact Publishers. Original ed., 1970.

Barlow, D. H., and Craske, N. G. (1994). *Mastery of Your Anxiety and Panic.* Albany, New York: Graywind Publications.

Beck, A. T. (1988). *Love Is Not Enough.* New York: Harper & Row.

Burns, D. D. (1999). *Feeling Good.* New York: Morrow.

Dryden, W. (1994). *Overcoming Guilt!* London: Sheldon Press.

Dryden, W., and Gordon, J. (1991). *Think Your Way to Happiness.* London: Sheldon Press.

Ellis, A. (2001). *How to Stubbornly Refuse to Make Yourself Miserable About Anything—Yes, Anything!* New York: Citadel Press.

———. (2000). *How to Control Your Anxiety Before It Controls You.* New York: Kensington Publishing.

———. (1999). *How to Make Yourself Happy and Remarkably Less Disturbable.* Atascadero, Cal.: Impact Publishers.

———. (2001). *Feeling Better, Getting Better, and Staying Better.* Atascadero, Cal.: Impact Publishers.

———. (2001). *Overcoming Destructive Beliefs, Feelings, and Behaviors.* Amherst, N.Y.: Prometheus Books.

Ellis, A., and Becker, I. (1982). *A Guide to Personal Happiness.* North Hollywood, Cal.: Melvin Powers.

Ellis, A., and Crawford, T. (2002). *Making Intimate Connections.* Atascadero, Cal.: Impact Publishers.

Ellis, A., and Harper, R. A. (1997). *A Guide to Rational Living.* North Hollywood, Cal.: Melvin Powers.

———. (1961). *A Guide to Successful Marriage.* North Hollywood, Cal.: Melvin Powers, Inc.

Ellis, A., and Knaus, W. (1977). *Overcoming Procrastination.* New York: New American Library.

Ellis, A., and Lange, A. (1994). *How to Keep People from Pushing Your Buttons.* New York: Carol Publishing Group.

Ellis, A. and Powers, M. G. (2000). *The Secret of Overcoming Verbal Abuse.* North Hollywood, Cal.: Melvin Powers.

Ellis, A., and Tafrate, R. C. (2000). *How to Control Your Anger Before It Controls You.* New York, N.Y.: Citadel Press.

Ellis A., and Velten, E. (1998). *Optimal Aging: Get Over Getting Older.* Chicago: Open Court Publishing.

———. (1992). *When AA Doesn't Work for You: Rational Steps for Quitting Alcohol.* New York: Barricade Books.

FitzMaurice, K. E. (1997). *Attitude Is All You Need.* Omaha, Neb.: Palm Tree Publishers.

Freeman, A., and DeWolf, R. (1989). *Woulda, Coulda, Shoulda.* New York: Morrow.

Glasser, W. (1999). *Choice Theory.* New York: Harper Perennial.

Hauck, P. A. (1991). *Overcoming the Rating Game: Beyond Self-Love— Beyond Self-Esteem.* Louisville, K.Y.: Westminster/John Knox.

Lazarus, A., and Lazarus, C. N. (1997). *The 60-Second Shrink.* Atascaclero, Cal.: Impact Publishers.

Lazarus, A., Lazarus, C., and Fay, A. (1993). *Don't Believe It for a Minute: Forty Toxic Ideas That Are Driving You Crazy.* Atascaclero, Cal.: Impact Publishers.

Low, A. A. (1952). *Mental Health Through Will Training.* Boston: Christopher.

Miller, T. (1986). *The Unfair Advantage.* Manlius, N.Y.: Horsesense, Inc.

Mills, D. (1993). *Overcoming Self-Esteem.* New York: Albert Ellis Institute.

Russell, B. (1950). *The Conquest of Happiness.* New York: New American Library.

Seligman, M. E. P. (1991). *Learned Optimism.* New York: Knopf.

Wolfe, J. L. (1992). *What to Do When He Has a Headache.* New York: Hyperion.

Young, H. S. (1974). *A Rational Counseling Primer.* New York: Albert Ellis Institute.

Index

About the Authors

ALBERT ELLIS, Ph.D., born in Pittsburgh and raised in New York City, holds M.A. and Ph.D. degrees in clinical psychology from Columbia University. He has held many important psychological positions, including Chief Psychologist of the State of New Jersey and adjunct professorships at Rutgers and other universities. He is currently president of the Albert Ellis Institute in New York City; has practiced psychotherapy, marriage and family counseling, and sex therapy for almost sixty years; and continues this practice at the Psychological Clinic of the Institute in New York. He is the founder of Rational Emotive Behavior Therapy (REBT) and the originator of modern Cognitive Behavior Therapy (CBT).

Dr. Ellis has served as president of the Division of Consulting Psychology of the American Psychological Association and of the Society for the Scientific Study of Sexuality, and as officer of several professional societies, including the American Association of Marital and Family Therapy, the American Academy of Psychotherapists, and the American Association of Sex Educators, Counselors, and Therapists. He is a diplomate in clinical psychology of the American Board of Professional Psychology and of several other professional boards.

Professional societies that have given Dr. Ellis their highest professional and clinical awards include the American Psychological Association, the Association for the Advancement of Behavior Therapy, the American Counseling Association, and the American Psychopathological Association. He was ranked as one of the "most influential psychologists" by both American and Canadian psychologists and counselors. He has served as consulting or associate editor of many scientific journals, and has published over 800 scientific papers and more than 200 audio and video cassettes. He has authored or edited over sixty-five books and monographs, including a number of best-selling popular and professional volumes.

ROBERT A. HARPER, Ph.D., was trained in psychology, anthropology, and sociology at Ohio State University and then took post-doctoral training in psychotherapy in Detroit, New York, and Washington. He has taught at several leading universities and directed counseling training programs at Ohio State University and the Merrill-Palmer Institute in Detroit.

Dr. Harper has been president of the American Academy of Psychotherapists and of the American Association for Marital and Family Therapy. He has also been president of several divisions of the American Psychological Association, including the Divisions of Counseling Psychology, the Division of Psychotherapy, and the Division of Humanistic Psychology. He was in private practice of psychotherapy and marriage and family counseling in Washington, D.C., for forty years. He has been given many awards and honors by a number of scientific and professional organizations, including the divisions of psychotherapy and of clinical psychology of the American Psychological Association.

Dr. Harper has written more than one hundred papers for professional and popular publications and is the author of several influential books, including *Marriage* and *Psychoanalysis and Psychotherapy: 36 Systems*. He is now retired but is quite active in his ninth decade and continues to enjoy many activities, of which gardening and travel are prominent.